WILD TRIBES IN INDIAN HISTORY

WILD TRIBES IN INDIAN HISTORY

B. A. SALETORE

GYAN

Published by

GYAN

Gyan Publishing House
5, Ansari Road
Daryaganj, New Delhi-110002
Phone: 011-47034999, 9811692060
E-mail: books@gyanbooks.com

Distribution Network
gyanbooks.com
India, USA, Canada, UK, Australia

ISBN:978-93-7097-135-6 (PB)
First Published, 1935

2nd Impression 2025

Printed at: Gyan Press, Delhi.

WILD TRIBES IN INDIAN HISTORY
Arthur B. A. SALETORE

THE WILD TRIBES IN INDIAN HISTORY

BY

Dr. B. A. Saletore, M. A., Ph. D., (Lond. et Giessen)

PROFESSOR OF HISTORY

SIR PARASHURAMBHAU COLLEGE

POONA

LAHORE

Motilal Banarsi Das

Panjab Sanskrit Book Depôt

1935

THE WILD TRIBES IN INDIAN HISTORY

BY

Dr. B. A. Saletore, M. A., Ph. D.,

PREFACE

The continual havoc which forest tribes caused in the Karṇāṭaka and Tamil lands in early and mediaeval times, made me enquire whether they were native only to the southern and western parts of India. The following work is the result of my investigations. Its aim is to give a short history of such of the tribes which, so far as the available information about them is concerned, have added to the annals of the country. Their activities have been described with special reference to the history of western and southern India, from the earliest times to the end of the eighteenth century A. D.

10th April 1935
198/11, Tilak Road
Poona 2

B. A. S.

CONTENTS

CORRIGENDA

Page	Line	For	Read
9	20	Choḍas	Coḍas
16	22	was	were
24	8	slughter	slaughter
25	9	elephans	elephants
25	16	Beḍar	Kirāta
30	13	shape	shapes
31	7	played	played with
64	8	serpant	serpent
72	28	Helagavatti	Beḷagavatti
80	23	Nāganda	Nāgaṇṇa
84	18	A. D. 1135	A. D. 1235
87	4	slove	solve
93	13	Kumāara	Kumara

THE WILD TRIBES IN INDIAN HISTORY

CHAPTER I

POLICY OF THE HINDU RULERS TOWARDS THE WILD TRIBES

Summary :— Nature of the subject – Sources of information-Ktesias on the policy of the Indian rulers towards the wild tribes–Kauṭalya's regulations–S'ukrācārya on the contingents of wild tribes and their corporations – As'oka's policy towards the wild tribes – Kṛṣṇa Deva Rāya's injunctions in regard to them.

Ever since the dawn of Indian history, statesmen and citizens alike have had to count on one turbulent element which caused them not only grave concern but oftentimes much peril as well. This was the presence of a great many wild tribes who, dispersed by the continual influx of superior and more cultured peoples, proved always to be a source of infinite danger to the State.[1] From earliest times Hindu legists and monarchs made, on the whole, conscious efforts more for enlisting the services of these disturbing factors than for exterminating them altogether from the land. Whether the marked sympathy which the rulers showed to the wild tribes was itself responsible for the continual havoc which the latter caused in the country, or whether it was a confession on the part of the kings to deal satisfactorily with the uncompromising agents of disorder who, both because of their insurmountable numbers and the nature of their inaccessible homes in the mountain fastnesses and forests of the land, eluded the clutches of law, one cannot say with definiteness, especially because of the paucity of materials dealing with this particular phase of the question. But it must be confessed that Hindu rulers did not always show the wild tribes consideration: when the latter stubbornly resisted the imperialistic designs of the former, they were conquered, and, in a few instances, annihilated.

The story of the significant part which the wild tribes have played in Indian history is gathered from a great many sources, the most prominent among which are literature, both Hindu and Buddhist, writings of foreign travellers, traditional accounts, and epigraphical records.

That the Hindu monarchs extended to the wild tribes their hand of friendship is clear from the observations of foreign writers. Ktesias, who calls them by the general appellation of Kynokephaloi (and also Kynomolgoi), describes them at some length.[2] He informs us that they stood in a free friendship with the Indian king. To him they brought annually two hundred and sixty talents of dried fruit of the Siptakhora tree on rafts, and as many talents of a red dye-stuff and one thousand of elektron or the gum exuding from the Siptakhora tree. To the Indians they sold their wares, and obtained from them in exchange bread, oatmeal, cotton clothes, bows, and lances, which they required in hunting and killing wild animals. Every fifth year the king presented them with three hundred bows, three thousand lances, one hundred and twenty thousand small shields, and fifty thousand swords.[3]

Evidently the Hindu kings reckoned them more than mere hunting agents in the wilds. Kauṭalya enlightens us on the question of the amity that existed between the kings and the wild tribes. Unlike the previous legists, who treated them under the general designation of Mlecchas, he calls them *araṇyacarāḥ*.[4] While describing the attitude of a conqueror, Kauṭalya relates the following:—" He should observe the policy of conciliation by promising the protection of villages, of those who live in forests....By instigating any one of a neighbouring king, a wild chief, a scion of the enemy's family, or an imprisoned prince, he should sow the seeds of dissension...Whoever helps him (the king) against his enemy, his enemy's ally, his neighbour, and wild tribes, is a friend affording enjoyment on all sides (sarvatobhogi).

" If he happens to have an enemy in the rear, or a wild chief, or an enemy, or a chief enemy capable of being propitiated with the gift of land, he should provide such an enemy with a useless piece of land...a wild chief with a piece of land yielding no livelihood..."

It was essential for a ruler to conciliate the wild tribes. Kauṭalya explains to us why such a policy of friendship was extended to them. They could cause greater harm to the State than robbers. In the *Artha-ṡāstra* we are told that "robbers carry off the property of the careless, and can be put down as they are easily recognized and caught hold of, whereas wild tribes have their own strongholds, being numerous and brave, ready to fight in broad daylight, and seizing and destroying countries like kings."[6]

The State, therefore, according to Kauṭalya, differentiated the wild tribes from the robbers. This is further proved by the careful manner in which Kauṭalya characterizes their depredations. He writes thus:—" Obstruction to movements caused by a chief is internal obstruction; and obstruction to movements caused by an enemy or wild tribe is external obstruction."[7] Then again–"The provocation of the chief of a district (rāṣṭramukhya), the officer in charge of the boundry, the chief of wild tribes, and a conquered is what is termed external trouble."[8]

In the conduct of a campaign the wild tribes were an element which the ruler had to reckon. Kauṭalya lays down the following injunction:— 'Finance, the army, the strength of the armies of friends, enemies, and wild tribes, the prospect of rains, and the seasons should be thoroughly examined."[9] Further we are told the following in the same work:- "...of strength, place, and time, each is helpful to the other; whoever is possessed of these three things should, after having placed one-third or one-fourth of his army to protect his base of operations against his rear enemy and wild tribes in his vicinity.......march during the month of Mārgas'īrṣa (December)......."[10]

Kauṭalya describes the time for the engagement of wild tribes thus:—"When he (the conqueror) thinks that he will have to make his strong enemy to fight against another enemy, on account of a city, a plain, or a wild tract of land, and that in that fight he will achieve one or the other of his objects......that through the battle he will have the mischievous power of his enemy's allies or of wild tribes destroyed......and that the time of battle between inferior kings has arrived, then is the time for the exercise of an enemy's forces."

"This explains the time for the engagement of wild tribes.

"When he thinks that the army of wild tribes is living by the same road (that his enemy has to traverse); that the road is unfavourable for the march of his enemy's army; that his enemy's army consists mostly of wild tribes......then is the time for engaging the army of wild tribes".

Wild tribes could certainly be incorporated in the State army. They could form one of the five armies which the king commanded. " When a king achieves this or that object with the assistance of a friend who is to receive the help of his army in return later on, then he may send out his various kinds of army- such as hereditary army, hired army, army formed of corporations of people, his friend's army, and the army composed of wild tribes- either that kind of army which has experience of all sorts of grounds and of seasons or the army of enemies or of wild tribes, which is far removed in space and time. "[12]

The contingent of wild tribes had to receive definite remuneration from the State. " Of these armies, one has to pay the army of wild tribes either with raw produce or with allowance for plunder. "[13]

But a contingent of wild tribes was by no means a unit on which the king could always rely. " The army of an enemy under the leadership of an Ārya is better than the army of wild tribes. Both of them (the army of an enemy and of wild tribes) are anxious for plunder. In the absence of plunder and under troubles, they prove as dangerous as a lurking snake. "[14]

Inspite of the distrust with which the king had to view the wild tribes, it was advisable to use them for the safety of the State. " This (*i. e.*, external danger) should be overcome by setting one against the other. Whoever among these has strongly fortified himself should be caught hold of through the agency of a frontier king or the chief of wild tribes...... "[15]

Further, the wild tribes were to be used against

one's own allies thus:—"When the ally has finished his work, he should, under some excuse, try to get back his army; or he may send to his ally that army which is composed of traitors, enemies, and wild tribes........"[16]

The regulations pertaining to the wild tribes as laid down by Kauṭalya were transmitted to the later generations as a part of the domestic policy of the Hindu rulers. We thus find the following injunctions in the political manual of S'ukrācārya concerning the different kinds of armies and the lattitude which the kings had to give to the corporations of wild tribes. There is every reason to believe that these latter, while they maintained their inherent wild nature and continued to be a source of infinite trouble to the State, gradually came under the more humane influence around them, especially in the ages when the *S'ukranīti* was composed. This we infer from what S'ukrācārya has to say in regard to them. While describing the manner in which a commander is to station his contingents, he says:— "The following are to be stationed in the order indicated below: first the lower officers and servants; then the commander; then infantry, then the cavalry, then the men of horse, men with elephants, then the guns and ordnances, then the mares, then the bodyguards and aides-de-camp, then the foresters."[17]

The different kinds of armies mentioned by S'ukrācārya are not the same as those mentioned by Kauṭalya. S'ukrācārya informs us that "The army regimented by the State and the regiments formed among soldiers themselves; likewise the army receiving conveyances from the State (or not). The Kirātas and people living in the forests who are dependent on their own resources and strength (belong to the latter class)"[18]

S'ukrācāry's broad-mindedness is seen in the provision he made to try the foresters. "The foresters are to be tried with the help of foresters, merchants by merchants, soldiers by soldiers, and in the village (affairs are to be administered) by persons who live with both parties (*i. e.*, neighbours)."[19]

India produced monarchs who went far ahead of the maxims which the lawgivers had enunciated concerning the treatment that was to be meted out to the wild tribes. With them the primary need was not that of entertaining the wild tribes in State service but of weaning them from their savage habits and of leading them along the path of progress. The most celebrated name in this field of national uplift is that of Aśoka. His Rock-Edicts prove beyond any doubt the profound character of the new policy he inaugurated. To him there was no distinction between his own and other people. In the I. separate Rock-Edict at Dhauli we read the following:— "All men are my children. As on behalf of (my own) children, I desire that they may be provided with complete welfare and happiness in this world and in the other world, the same I desire also on behalf of (all) men."[20] In the II. Rock-Edict at Shāhbazgarhi, we find a clue to the motive which may be said to underly such a noble declaration:—"But whatever effort king Devānampriya Priyadars'in is making, all that (is) only for the sake of (merit) in the other (world), (and) in order that all (men) may be free of danger."[21]

Inspite of this charter of impartiality, As'oka seems to have shown marked consideration to the border-land people. The II. separate Rock-Edict at Dhauli tells us what exactly Aśoka intended to convey in regard to the wild tribes who lived on the borders of his vast

Empire. "It might occur to (my) unconquered borderers (to ask): 'What does the king desire with reference to us?' (This) alone is my wish with reference to the borderers, that they may learn that Devānampriya... that they may not be afraid of me, but may have confidence (in me); that they may obtain only happiness from me, not misery; that they may (learn) this: that Devānampriya will forgive them, what can be forgiven; that they may (be induced by me to) practise morality; (and) that they may attain (happiness in) this world and (in) the other world. For the following purpose I am instructing you, (*viz*., that) I may discharge the debt (which I owe to them), by this, that I instruct (you) and inform (you) of (my) will, *i. e.*, my unshakable resolution and vow.

"Therefore, acting thus, you (*i. e.*, Māhāmātrās) must fulfil (your) duty, and must inspire confidence to them, in order that they (*i. e.*, the border-land people) may learn that Devānampriya is to them like a father, that Devānampriya loves them like himself, and that they are to Devānampriya like his own children."[22]

And of the border people, the wild tribes living in the forests received particular favour at the hands of the monarch. A great law was passed regarding the safety of the inhabitants of the forests. "Forests must not be burnt, either uselessly or in order to destroy (living beings)"—so runs an order in the V. Pillar Edict at Delhi.[23] The success which crowned his efforts in this direction can be seen from the statements made in more than one Rock-Edict. The XIII. Rock-Edict at Shāhbazgarhi relates the following:— "And even (the inhabitants of) the forests which are (included) in the dominions of Devānampriya, even those he pacifies and converts."[24] In the same Rock-Edict he informs us that "Likewise here in the king's territory, among the Yonas and Kāmboyas, among the Nabhakas and Nabhitis, among the Bhojas and Pitinikas, among the Āndhras and Palidas—everywhere (people) are conforming to Devānampriya's instruction in morality." [25]

The Rock-Edicts do not, it must be confessed, enlighten us on the particular names of the wild tribes who form the subject of this treatise. Nevertheless from the name of one of the many tribes dealt with in the above Rock-Edict – the Āndhras–, we may conclude that Aśoka must have bestowed equal care on the other wild tribes whom he does not mention in his edicts. The Āndhras in the early ages were, as we shall see later on, according to Manu, a barbarous race; and we can only assume that the other kindred wild tribes must also have come in for their share of the monarch's unrivalled magnanimity. If, as the II. Rock-Edict at Shāhbazgarhi relates, "Everywhere in the dominions of Devānampriya Priyadarśin, and (of those) who (are his) borderers, such as the Choḍas, the Pāṇḍyas, the Satiyaputra, the Keralaputra, the Tāmrapaṇṇi,...everywhere two–2–(kinds of) medicinal treatment were established by Devānampriya Priyadarśin...." [26], it is not unlikely that the diligent emissaries (*i. e.*, the Mahāmātrās) entrusted with the duty of instructing the people in morality *everywhere*,[27] did not fail to give moral and material succour to the numerous wild tribes whose assistance, as we shall prove latter on, had been sought by no less a personage than the founder of the Maurya dynasty himself, and who had spread far and wide in the Empire of As'oka.

As'oka's principles concerning the wild tribes came to stay in the country. How far his immediate successors followed his instructions, it is difficult to say for the present. But ages after the Mauryan Empire had crumbled, famous Karṇāṭaka monarchs gave vent to similar views in regard to the wild tribes who had caused considerable damage to the kingdoms of southern India. One of them was the Hoysala king Vinayāditya Deva, whose diplomatic dealings with the wild tribes have been briefly described in epigraphs to which we shall advert later on in the course of this treatise. Another monarch who has written at some length on the same subject is Kṛṣṇa Deva Rāya the Great of Vijayanagara. In his well known work called *Āmuktamālyada*, he has detailed the procedure which was meant for his own guidance as well as that of his successors. Kṛṣṇa Deva Rāya the Great was a monarch who was intimately acquainted with the habits of the wild tribes. He took a lesson even from the Ābhiras and the Bhills. In the above work he says:— " It is essential that a king should be able to enforce his commands. Even the Ābhiras and the Bhills of the forests are able to enforce their orders, as by the sign of the arrow and the piece of thread. Much more is it necessary that an emperor (*sārvabhauma*) should be able to enforce his command. "[28] Then again,—" When the foresters promise to do anything after partaking of food mixed with milk in any man's house, they would under no circumstances swerve from their promise. If they observe any wrong, however small it might be, they would become angry and become enemies without considering the probable results of their action. "[29]

The Vijayanagara monarch was not averse to the wild tribes living within their own fastnesses so long as they did not prove a danger to his Government. He says thus in his work :— " Increase the forests that are near your frontier fortresses (gaḍi-des'a) and destroy all those which are in the middle of your territory. Then alone you will not have trouble from robbers."

On the question of controlling the wild tribes, the Emperor writes thus :—" It is always advisable to entrust the government over wild tribes inhabiting hills and forests to heroes who have fallen from great positions. It would not affect the king much whoever succeeds in the struggle between them."[31] The Emperor further remarks thus :—"The first wild tribes can be brought under control by truthfulness (keeping one's engagements with them)..."[32]

In the above observations as well as in the following one, there is clear evidence of the Emperor's compassion and sincerity towards the wild tribes, which we noticed in the promulgations of As'oka. "If the people of the forest (wild tribes)," writes Kṛṣṇa Deva Rāya, "multiply in any state, the trouble to the king and his people would not be small. The king should make such people his own by destroying their fears. Because they are people of very little advancement, faith and want of faith, anger and friendship, bitter enmity and close friendship, result from (very little) insignificant causes.

"When a forester (Bhill) went with his bow to another's house, the other entertained him with food mixed in milk, he observed the bark of some tree boiling on the fire-place for making ropes and mistook it for flesh. Angry because he was not entertained with the flesh, the forester resolved to murder his host when he came to give him a send-off. But on that occasion the latter excused himself from following further saying that the fibre on the fire-place would get spoiled. The man understood his mistake and parted with his host heartily. Do you not know this story ?......Minding the (small) faults of the forest chiefs who have not extensive power is like trying to clean a mud wall by pouring water over it. If he gets angry at them he cannot destroy them utterly. If (on the other hand) he attaches them to himself by kind words and charity, they would be useful to him in invading foreign territory and plundering their fortresses. It is inconceivable that a king would be able to meet a hundred faults with a thousand punishments."[33] The non-observance of these noble maxims of Kṛṣṇa Deva Rāya the Great by his successors had a profound effect on the life of the powerful mediaeval Hindu Empire.

CHAPTER II

THE KIRĀTAS

Summary:— Indentification – Original home: foreign travellers' opinion confirmed by notices in Hindu epics and *Purāṇas* – Spread to the north, the north-west, the west, and the south – Description – Faith: their contribution to the Hindu religion – As historical factors: from the times of the *Mahābhārata* till the end of the seventeenth century A. D.

A great many septs comprised the wild tribes whom, as we remarked in the previous pages, Hindu rulers and legists were inclined to view with consideration and sympathy. It may reasonably be maintained that the wild tribes contained peoples of different races. This may to some extent explain why, as narrated above, Hindu lawgivers included under the general category of Mlecchas diverse peoples, some of whom, like the Yonas, as is well known, were civilized nations. To the indiscrimination which the earlier writers made between foreign peoples who were by no means barbarous, and indigenous tribes of non-Indian extraction, we have to add another difficulty which prevents us from delineating the history of all or most of the wild tribes of India. This is the close resemblance which one sect of wild tribes bore to another and the consequent confusion in the accounts of Hindu writers in their description of these peoples. These limitations together with the paucity of materials dealing with those tribes not mentioned in this treatise, make it impossible for us to give a more thorough history of all the wild tribes who have figured in the annals of the land.

Of those particular tribes, however, about whom we have interesting details both in the accounts of foreign travellers and Hindu writers, prominence may be given to the Kirātas. Manu opines that the Kirātas together with other peoples were Kṣatriyas, and that they became degraded because of the extinction of sacred rites :—

> S'anakaiḥ-tu kriyālopādimāḥ Kṣatriyajātayaḥ ।
> Vṛis'alatvaṃ gatā loke Brāhmaṇa adars'anena-ca ॥
> Pauṇḍrakāḥ-ca-Oḍra-Drāviḍāh Kāmbojā Yavanāḥ S'akāḥ ।
> Pāradāḥ-Pallavāḥ Cīnāḥ Kirātā Daradāḥ Khas'āḥ ॥[1]

We cannot agree with the verdict of some that this statement of Manu reflects the opinion of a later age,[2] since in the *Mahābhārata* too we find a detailed explanation of Manu's definition on two different occasions. We are told in that epic that the Mekalas, the Drāviḍas the Lāṭhas, the Pauṇḍras, the Konavas'iras, the Cauṇḍikas, the Daradas, the Darvas, the Cauras, the S'abaras, the Barbaras, the Kirātas, the Yavanas, and numerous other tribes of the Kṣatriyas were degraded to the status of S'ūdras through the wrath of the Brāhmaṇs. Then, again, we are informed the following in the *Asvamedha Parva*:- On Rāma (son of Jamadagni) destroying the army of Karttavīrya, some of the Kṣatriyas, afflicted with the terror of Jamadagni's son, entered mountain fastnesses, like deer afflicted by the lion. Of them that were unable, through the fear of Rāma, to discharge the duties ordained for their order, the progeny became Vṛis'āls owing to their inability to find Brāhmaṇas. In this way the Drāviḍas and Ābhiras and Puṇḍras together with the S'abaras became Vṛis'ālas through hose men who had Kṣatriya duties assigned to them (in consequence of their birth), falling away (from their) duties.

The same epic enlightens us on the wide use of the the term Kṣatriya: The Kirātas, the Dar(a)das, the Darvas, the Ṣurus, the Vaiyāmakas, the Auḍumvars, the Durvibhāgas, the Pāradas, along with the Bāhlikas, the Kāśmīras, the Kumāras, the Ghorakas, the Haṅsakayanas, the S'ivis, the Trigartas, the Yaudheyas, the ruler of the Madras, and the Kaikeyas, the Amvastas, the Kaukuras, the Tarkṣyas, the Vastrapas, along with the Pahlavas, the Vaṣātyās, the Mauleyas, the Kṣudrakas, the Mālavas, the Paṇḍryas, the Sānavatyas, and the Gayas,—these good and well-born Kṣatriyas distributed into regular classes and trained to the use of arms, brought tribute into king Yudhiṣṭira by hundreds and thousands.

But it is clear from the remarks of Kṛṣṇa in an earlier connection that these Kṣatriyas were of tainted origin. Kṛṣṇa tells Yudhiṣṭira the following:— I shall, however, still tell thee something. Those persons in the world that now go by the name of Kṣatriyas are inferior (in everything) to those Kṣatriyas that Rāma, the son of Jamadagni, exterminated.[3]

Whatever may be the interpretation given to the above explanation of the reduction of certain classes of people from a higher to a lower social level, there cannot be a doubt that in classical times the term Kṣaṭriya was applied to those of approved volour and ferocity, even though they were of distinct non-Indian origin; and that it was not restricted to a particular caste or sect of people who were entrusted with the sole duty of fighting and governing the country. We may bear this in mind, since it will elucidate a very interesting detail concerning the origin of one of the most famous reigning families of ancient India.

We may proceed with the question of the identification of the Kirātas. McCrindle identified them with the Chirotisagi (Chisiotosagi) mentioned by Megasthenes as living on the hills, the Scyrites of Pliny, and the Kirrhadai of the *Periplus Mari Erythræ*. He also rightly remarked that they were of Mongolian origin.[4] But his indentification of the Airrhadoi of Ptolemy with the Kirātas,[5] has been rejected by Gerini who would place them not along the Ganges river but on the eastern coast of the Gulf of Bengal from the mouth of the Bṛahmaputṛā down to that of the Nāf.[6] According to Gerini, the people of Tipperah, Kacā, and Silhet (Sylhet) were Kirātas.[7]

Hindu epics and *Purāṇas* substantiate the above surmise that the Kirātas were originally of eastern extraction. In the course of his eastern wanderings, Bhīma sent expeditions from Videha, and conquered seven kings of the Kirātas living about the Indra mountain.[8] We are also told in the same epic that the unassailable troops of Bhagadatta was crowded with the Cins and Kirātas, all looking like figures of gold and assuming a beauty like that of a forest of *karṇikāra* trees.[9] A similar statement coupling the Cins with the Kirātas is made in another connection where we are told that Arjuna attacked the kingdom of Prāgjyotiśa, and that the king of Prāgjyotiśa was supported by a host of Kirātas and Cins and other warriors who dwelt by the sea-coast.[10] It is not unlikely that the Cins and the Kirātas were associated together because of their common Mongolian origin.

From the *Mahābhārata* we learn that there were many tribes among the Kirātas. Kṛṣṇa beholding the sons of Pṛitha dressed in deep skins, became filled with rage, and addressing Yudhiṣṭira said that at the *rājasūya* sacrifice performed at Indraprastha, he (Kṛṣṇa) had seen all kings of the mainland, the islands, the countries on the sea-board, the frontier states, and " all the chiefs of the sea coast and the kings of the Pahlavas and the Daradas and the various tribes of the Kirātas and Yavanas and Cakras " and others who performed various offices on that memorable occasion.[11] In the *sabhā* numerous kings waited on Yudhiṣṭira. Among them were Pulinda and Sumans, two kings of the Kirātas. "[12]

In the topographical list of the peoples given in the same epic as well as in the *Purāṇas* we have, on the whole, the fact of the Kirātas being located in the east. But it may be remembered that from the same works we can gather that by the time they were composed, the Kirātas had sought fresher fields of activity in the north and north-west of India. The diverse tribes of the Kirātas are mentioned in the *Mahābhārata* after the Poṣakas and the Kaliṅgas and before the Tomaras, the Haṁsamārgas, and the Karamanjakas. The kingdoms of these peoples are described to be in the east and north.[13] In the same context they are classed together with the Puṇḍras, the Bhārgas, the Sudeṣanas, the Kuruvarṇakas, and the Barbaras.[14]

The eastern home of the Kirātas is further proved by the statements in the *Viṣṇu Purāṇa*. On the east of Bhārata dwell the Kirātas, on the west, the Yavanas-so says the *Viṣṇu Purāṇa*.[15] In another passage we are told that to the north of the Mahi(Mahya)uttaras, were the Prāviṣeyas, the Bhārgavas, the Puṇḍras, and the Kirāta .[16]

The *Mārkaṇḍeya Purāṇa*, while it confirms the statement of the *Viṣṇu Purāṇa* regarding the eastern habitat of the Kirātas, also speaks of them as living in other directions, suggesting thereby that they had already begun to seek newer homes across the continent. While describing the nine divisions of the country, the *Mārkaṇḍeya Purāṇa* relates that the Jambudvīpa is a thousand *yojanas* in length from south to north. At its eastern end are the Kirātas and at its west, the Yavanas.[17]

The *Agni Purāṇa* has a similar account to give of the nine divisions of Bharatavarṣa and of the peoples who occupied them. It says that the length of the land from north to south was eight thousand miles; and that reckoned from the east were the land of the Kirātas, the land of the Yavanas, and the land of the Brāhmaṇas.[18]

From the manner in which the Kirātas are described in the *Mārkaṇḍeya Purāṇa*, it is clear that when that work was composed, they had already scattered themselves on the northern, western, and even southern sides of the land. In one connection the *Mārkaṇḍeya Purāṇa* describes them to be between the Animadras and the Tāmasas.[19] Their country is spoken of in the same *Purāṇa* as resting against the mountains.[20] Further, they are said to be a people who were " situated in the right-hand foot " of the Tortoise.[21] Then, again, one class of the Kirātas called the Adhama, or the rudest and basest races of the Kirātas, is located in the Tortoise's left flank.[22] They are also mentioned as living in the Tortoise's north-east foot.[23]

These remarks of the *Mārkāṇḍeya Purāṇa*, especially those relating to the Kirātas being situated in the " right-hand foot " (of the Tortoise , far from being "improbable" and "out of place," as Pargiter remarked,[24] may be accepted as valid in so far as they point out the directions in which the Kirātas had dispersed ever since the times of the *Mahābhārata*. From the above accounts in the *Mārkaṇḍeya Purāṇa*, we are to understand that they had now inhabited probably the southern part of the Aravali Hills, and certainly the regions of the Vindhyan forests.

The *Matsya Purāṇa* corroborates our surmise. Accepting the confusion which the earlier writers made concerning the Mlecchas and the wild tribes, it relates that the former lived on the outskirts of Bharatavarṣa, the Kirātas inhabiting the east, and the Yavanas the west of it.[25] But while describing the various *janapadas* situated on the banks of the rivers of India, the *Matsya Purāṇa* remarks that in the *madhya-deśa*, or central regions, were the *janapadas* of the Bhadrakāsas, the Vāhyas, Paṭṭacaras, Matsyas, Kirātas, Kulyas, and the like.[26] More details concerning the exact location of the kingdoms of the Kirātas are given in a later passage where it is stated that the *Aryan janapadas* of the Kirātas and the Pulindas were watered by the sacred Ganges which striking against the Vindhyan hills falls into the Hlādinī Ganges. The Hlādinī Ganges is described in the same context as running east ward into the sea after passing through the countries of Upaka, Niṣāda, Kirāta, Kālañjara, and others.[27] The same *Purāṇa* relates that the Kirāta kingdom was situated on the mountains.[28]

Further notices in the *Purāṇas* and the *kāvyas* strengthen our belief that by the sixth century A. D., the Kirātas had not only colonized the Himālayas, the Panjab but also the Vindhyan forests. These last came to be associated with them in the works of the

Hindu writers. The *Brihatsamhita* locates them in the south-west as well as in the north-east division.[29] Kālidāsa places them on the Himālayas; and Bāṇa, in the eastern regions. After the subjugation of the Pāraśikas and the Yavanas in the west, Raghu proceeded in a northerly direction. Halting for a while on the banks of the Sindhu, he conquered the Hūṇas (of the Panjab), broke the power of the Kāmbojas and the lord of the Kośalas. Then escorted by his cavalry, he reached the top of the mountain Himavat. Here his soldiers rested for a while. At the halting places left by Raghu the *devadāru* trees, whose barks had been bruised in places where the neck-ropes had been tied, indicated to the Kirātas the heights of the elephants. A battle ensued between the hill tribes and the forces of Raghu. The mountain tribes were subjugated. It is in this connection that Kālidāsa gives us the names of two classes of wild tribes whom his hero had conquered: they were the Utsvasaṅketas and the Kinnaras.[30]

That even in the times of Bāṇa the eastern regions were associated with the Kirātas is proved by the following description of Candrāpīḍa's world-conquest in the *Kādambarī*. Candrāpīḍa directed his forces eastwards and conquered and occupied Suvarṇapura, not far from the eastern Ocean, the abode of those Kirātas that dwell near Kailāsa, and who were called Hemajakūṭas.[31]

We may continue our remarks on the diffusion of the Kirātas in the southern and western regions of India, before we allude to their traces in the country today. In the age of the *Mahābhārata* itself they had occupied the western coast. This is proved by the following statements in that epic. Arjuna's white steeds yoked to his car, proceeded along the southern direction. The sacrificial horse entered the beautiful city of the Cedis called after the oyster (S'uktimatī) by S'arabha (the son of S'iśupāla). The steed then proceeded to the realm of the Kās'is, the Aṅgas, the Kos'alas, the Kirātas and the Taṅganas.[32]

More substantial evidence of the Kirātas having settled in the south is given in the account of Nakula's conquests. He reduced the fierce Mlecchas residing on the sea-coast as also the wild tribes of the Pahlavas, the Kirātas, the Yavanas, and the S'akas.[33]

The Niṣādas, who are spoken of as having been conquered by Sahadeva in the course of his southern conquests, were evidently a tribe kindred to the Kirātas, although, it must be confessed, we are unable for the present to point out the lines of resemblance between the two kinds of wild tribes. We may note, however, that in the passage under question Sahadeva is said to have conquered first the S'ūrasenas, then the Adhirājas, next the kings Sukumāra and Sumitra, then the Matsyas, the Paṭaccharas, next the country of the Niṣādas and also the high hill called Gos'riṅga and that lord of the earth known as S'reṇimat.[34]

In the seventh century and after the Vindhyas were reputed to be the home of the Kirātas. We shall presently cite the evidence of Daṇḍin, the author of *Daśakumāracarita*, in connection with this assertion of ours. Another equally well known writer, Paṃpā, who wrote the Kannaḍa work called *Vikramārjunavijaya* or *Paṃpā Bhārata* in the S'aka year 863 (A. D. 941), introduces the Kirātas as messengers (*Kirāta-dūtaṃ*) who inform Dharmarāja of the movements of Duryodhana.[35] In an equally celebrated work called *Paṃpā Rāmāyaṇa*, by a later writer named

Abhinava Paṃpa (twelfth century A. D.), the Kirātas are located on the Vindhyas. Vālakhilya, the ruler of the town of Kuravakas, is taken prisoner by Raudrabhūti, a Mleccha king of the Vindhyan forests, with the aid of countless army of Kirātas.[36] Nijaguṇayogi, a Kannaḍa lexicographer of the later times, in his *Vivekacintāmaṇi*, mentions a Kirāta kingdom.[37]

The Kirātas have not at all disappeared from the history of India. They are called today Kirātis or Kirāntis; and they inhabit the southern slopes of the Himālayas and the eastern mountains, especially the Kirānt-des'a or the mountainous country lying between the Dud-Kosi and the Karki rivers in Nepāl. The term includes the Khambhu, Limbu, and Yākhā tribes. The Danaūr, Hayu and Thāmi tribes also claim to be Kirāntis, although their claim is disputed by the first three which are superior.[38] The *Rājamālā*, or the analytical account of the royal family of Tipperah (Skt. Tripura), states that the ancient name of Tipperah was Kirāta. The people of Tripura, according to some, were of the same origin as those of the Kācāris. It may incidentally be observed here that the medicinal plant *ciretta* is a corruption of Kirāta. This plant which is also called *anārya-tikta* (the bitter of the non-Āryans), grows in the lower regions of the Himālayas which form the country of the modern Kirānti.[39]

The term Kirāta is also applied to the tract from Bankut to Devagarh as well as to the western part of Gondwāna which, however, is distinguished by the appellation of Kirāta-Canda.[40]

Kirātapur in the Panjab is associated with the activities of Har Govind and Har Rai, the *gurus* of the Sikhs.[41] Grierson identified Garhwal and Kumaun with the districts mentioned in the *Mahābhārata* as containing settlements of the Kirātas.[42]

Hindu writers have portrayed the Kirātas in some detail. The *Rāmāyaṇa* describes them as dwelling in islands, wearing thick top-knots, and subsisting on raw fish.[43]

The *Mahābhārata* contains more picturesque descriptions of the Kirātas. Among the numerous tributary kings who paid tribute to Yudhiṣṭira were numberless chiefs of the Kirātas armed with cruel weapons, ever engaged in cruel deeds, eating fruits and roots, attired in skins, and living on the northern slopes of the Himavat and the region of the Kāruṣa on the sea-coast and on both sides of the Lohitya mountains. Although they had brought with them as tribute loads of sandal wood and aloe and also black aloe, heaps upon heaps of valuable skins and gold and perfumes, ten thousand serving girls of their own race, many beautiful animals and birds of remote countries, and much gold of great splendour procured from mountains, yet they had to wait at the gate being refused at first permission to enter.[44]

Sātyaki tells Yudhiṣṭira that he is eager to follow Arjuna, and gives an account of the army through which he has got to cut his way. " Crushing these in battle for thy good, O Pāṇḍava, I shall then follow the track of Savyasācin. Those other elephants, O King, seven hundred in number, that thou seest, all cased in armour and ridden by Kirātas, and decked with ornaments, the king of the Kirātas, desirous of his life, had formerly presented to Savyasācin, together with many servants in their train. These, O King, were formerly employed in doing thy business. Behold the vicissitudes that time brings about, for these are now battling against thee ! Those elephants are ridden by

Kirātas difficult of defeat in battle. They are accomplished in fighting from elephants, and are all sprung from the race of Agni. Formerly they were all vanquished in battle by Savyasācin. They are now waiting for me carefully, under the orders of Duryodhana. Slaying with my shafts, O King, these Kirātas difficult of defeat in battle, I shall follow in the track of Arjuna who is intent on the slughter of the ruler of the Sindhus. Those (other) huge elephans, sprung from the race of Añjana, of impenetrable hides, well trained, and adown whose cheeks and from whose mouths' the juicy secretions are trickling down, and which are well trained with armour and wholly of gold, are very effective in battle and resemble Airāvat himself ! They have come from the northern hills and are ridden by fierce robbers, that are of strong limbs, that are all foremost of warriors, and that are cased in steel coats of mail. There, amongst them, are persons born of the cow, or of the ape, or of diverse other creatures including those born of men. That division of the assembled Mlecchas that are all sinful and that come from the fastnesses of Himavat, seems at a distance to be of smoky colour. "[45]

The unnatural origin of some of the races of the Kirātas given in the above long and interesting description by Sātyaki, may have been perhaps only another mode of expressing what Megasthenes says in his account of the Kirātas, whom he calls Skiratai, and whose country he locates beyond India. According to him, they were snub-nosed, either because in the tender years of infancy their nostrils were pressed down, and continued to be so throughout their after lives; or because such was the natural shape of their organ.[46]

The Kirātas in the forests of the Vindhyas mentioned by Daṇḍin, referred to above, were Brāhman renegades, who had taken to the savage life of the foresters (*vanacarāḥ*). The son of one of these, by name Mātaṅga, gives us an account of what he used to do:—With a party of the Kirātas, he used to harass the neighbouring villagers, bring them to the forest, imprison them there and lead a life of lawlessness.[47] A humane leader of the mountaineers (*Kirāta-bhartṛi*) is mentioned in a later connection in the same work.[48] Daṇḍin also describes an intelligent (Kirāta) forest messenger who sold tiger skins and leather bags and gathered news as well in the city of Māhiśmatī.[49]

For a description of the Kirāta women we go to the Kannaḍa poet Vīrabhadrarāja (circa A. D. 1530) who writes thus:—

The Beḍar women resembled the flamingos in their movements, the cuckoos in their tone, the parrots in their speech, the ruddy geese (or Brāhmany ducks) in their breasts, and the peacocks in the beauty of their braids. Their claims for being considered as *vijāti* are (thus) intelligible because they possessed the charms of the (above) birds:—

naḍege-arasu-sañceyaṃ sarake kokilamaṃ bagevattu torppma mo- |
l-nuḍige s'ukaṅgalaṃ kuca-yugaṅgaḷa permmege jakka-vakiyaṃ ||
muḍige naviglaḷ-andavane poltu Kirāta-nitambinī-janaṃ |
biḍade vijāti-embudu-adu sārthakam-āgi-esed-irppudu-āvagam ||[50]

The most abiding gift which the Kirātas gave to the country was in the shape of a new deity to the Hindu pantheon. From epigraphical records as well as literature we know that the goddess whom the Kirātas and the kindred tribes worshipped was Caṇḍikā. Now, Caṇḍikā is, as is well known, no other than Durgā in the fierce form she assumed when she killed the demon Mahiṣa. The origin of Caṇḍikā or Durgā is similar to that of Tārā Bhagavatī, the celebrated Buddhist goddess of the Mahāyāna school. Tārā, as we shall describe in another work,* was born in the Tibetan regions. The origin of Durgā or Caṇḍikā, as given in the *Devī Māhātmyā* quoted in the *Mārkeṇḍeya Purāṇa,* [51] also leads us to suppose that this goddess too was born in those regions. The *Devī Māhātmyā* relates that on Asura Mahiṣa becoming Indra, the gods in fear ran to Viṣṇu and S'iva. From these two issued forth great energy which gathering into one form became a female. This was Caṇḍikā or Durgā. [52] In other words, according to the Śāktās, Durgā is the female principle in the universe-the embodiment of the *tejas* or energy of the gods, the other goddesses being merely her froms.

She is the *śakti* of Śiva; Tārā Bhagavatī is her counterpart and is the *śakti* of Avalokites'vara. [53]

Durgā or Caṇḍikā is praised in the *Mārkaṇḍeya Purāṇa* as protecting people from all evils. [4] In other words, she is a savioures. This is exactly the nature of Tārā Bhagavatī in Mahāyāna Buddhism. [55]

Just as Durgā is represented to be the mother of the gods, so also is Tārā described in the Mahāyāna texts to be the mother of the Buddhas as well as of the Boddhisattvas. [56]

Durgā is Kālī, the first of the Mahāvidyās. And Tārā is the second of the Mahāvidyas. Tārā, Durgā, and Kālī, according to the S'āktās, are one and the same.

Scholars are of opinion that the Indo-Aryans worshipped at first the male spirit, the adoration of the highly developed *s'akti* or female spirit coming in later. It is not denied that the worship of the latter was to a

* See the wirter's forth-coming book on Buddhism.

certain extent known to the Vedic Aryans. The question with which we are concerned is, firstly, which of the two forms is older– that of Durgā or Tārā; and who was responsible for the popularization of this essentially Kirāta deity in India. We say that Durgā or Caṇḍikā was primarily a Kirāta deity not merely from the fact of the place of the origin of this goddess being located more or less in the Kirānta-des'a we have described above, but also from the activities of a celebrated Buddhist teacher in Tibet as well as in India. This was Nāgārjuna, who has been assiged to the first or second century of the Christian era. We shall not go into the details of the history of this great Buddhist theologian but merely record the opinion that he, a southerner, revived the worship of Ēkajaṭā among the Bhoṭas of Tibet.[57] Ēkajaṭā is another name for Tārā Bhagavatī.

That the worship of Tārā existed already in Tibet (and in the Kirānta-des'a) before the advent of Nāgarjuna is a point which cannot be disputed. He was chiefly instrumental in popularizing that goddess in India. He propitiated Caṇḍikā and she submitted to him and agreed to supply the great monastery at Nāḷanda with provisions at his bidding. He fixed her in a thick pointed wooden club. She used to perform all the duties ascribed to her in the form of a beautiful woman. But, as the tradition goes, the chief cook of the monastery fell in love with her and burning the wooden club, set her at liberty.[58]

Whatever may be the truth attached to this tradition, we,have the fact of Nāgārjuna being a great propounder of Tāntrism and of his having made famous the adoration of Tārā. It is generally accepted that the Tāntric mode of worship introduced from Tibet either in the second century A. D. or a little later reached its zenith in the sixth and seventh centuries when the cult of Tārā spread far beyond the shores of India to the distant islands in the southern seas. We have no evidence to prove that prior to the age when Tārā was introduced from Tibet, there existed her Brahmanical counterpart Caṇḍikā or Durgā among the deities of the Hindus. We have seen above that it was somewhere in the sixth century or thereabouts that the Kirātas moved gradually from their eastern and northern homes towards the Aravali Hills and especially in the direction of the Vindhyan forests. We can only assume that consequent on their dispersion over the western and southern parts of Āryavarta, their deity too must have perambulated till she was admitted into the fold of the Hindu divinities and raised to the status of a premier goddess. The Buddhist Tārā was only the precursor, both in the matter of time and homage, of the Brahmanical Caṇḍikā or Durgā, although the *Devī Māhātmyā*, a work which has been assigned to the seventh century A. D.[59], would make us believe that the latter deity was of independent origin.

These suppositions of ours may be questioned but it cannot be denied that Caṇḍikā or Durgā was intrinsically a Kirāta deity. This we gather from Daṇḍin and Bāṇa. The former describes the Kirātas in a beautiful temple of Caṇḍikā ready to sacrifice a fair child to ensure success of their wild deeds. They say among themselves :— "We shall kill him with a sword suspending him by the branch of a tree, or by means of of a number of sharp arrows aimed at him after fixing his feet by digging (a hole) in the surface of sand, or by causing young dogs to kill as he will be running on all fours." Then, again, the name which Daṇḍin gives to Durgā in a later passage -that of Vindhyāvāsinī- only confirms our surmise that Caṇḍikā was the favourite deity of the Kirātas who had made the Vindhyan forests their home. King Tuṅgadhanvā of Suhma, desirous of securing progeny, solicited by prayers from Vindhyāvāsinī — who, by the way, forgetting her passion for a residence on the Vindhyā, had gone to Suhma - two children. The goddess appeared to him in a dream as he slept before her without food, and said, among other things, that he would get one son and one daughter, and that the latter was to worship the goddess every month on the Kṛittikā day by playing at ball in public.[60]

This statement of Daṇḍin is corroborated by the author of *Harivaṁśa* who tells us that surrounded by cocks, goats, lambs, lions, and tigers, and worshipped by the ringing of bells, Nārāyaṇī-which is another name for Durgā-adored by the S'abaras, Barbaras, and Pulindas, always lives on the mount Vindhya.[61]

The great S'abara leader who was a devout worshipper of Durgā, figuring in Bāṇa's *Kādambarī*, will presently be described.

The goddess Caṇḍikā whom the Kirātas thus worshipped, has also been described in detail in the *Devi Māhātmyā* referred to above, and in the *Kādambarī* of Bāṇa. We are told in the former that the bearer of the Pināka drawing a trident from his own trident gave it to her; and Kṛṣṇa gave a discus pulling it out from his discus. Varuṇa gave her a conch, Agni, a spear, Maruta, a bow, and a quiver filled with arrows. Indra, the lord of the immortals, gave her a thunderbolt pulling it out from his own thunderbolt, the thousand eyed gave her a bell from his elephant Airāvata. Yama gave her a rod from his own rod of

Fate; and the lord of the waters, a noose; Prajāpati presented her with a necklace of beads; Brahmā, an earthen pot; the Sun bestowed on her his own rays on all the pores of her skin. And Destiny gave her a sword and a spotless shield, and the Ocean of Milk, a spotless necklace of pearls and also a pair of undecaying garments. And a celestial crest-jewel, a pair of ear-rings, and bracelets, and a brilliant half-moon ornament, and armlets over all her arms, and also a pair of bright anklets, a necklet of the finest make and rings and gems on all her fingers–these Vis'vakarma gave her and also a brightly polished axe, weapons of many shape and also armour that could not be pierced. And Ocean gave her a garland of fadeless lotus flowers for her head and another for her breast and a very brilliant lotus flower besides. Himavat gave her a lion to ride on and gems of various kinds. Kubera gave her a drinking cup full of wine. Honoured by other gods also with gifts of ornaments and weapons, the goddess uttered a loud roar blendend with a horse-laugh again and again.[62]

Such was evidently the goddess Durgā in the temple where Vilāsvatī, as described in the *Kādambarī*, desirous of getting a child slept. That temple was dark with the smoke of bdellium ceaselessly burnt. But Bāṇa has a more detailed description to give of the temple of Durgā in another connection. Candrāpīḍa returning from Hemakūṭa to his father's palace, beheld on the way a red flag in a forest, near which was a shrine of Durgā guarded by an old Dravidian hermit who had made his abode thereby. The temple had a door made of the tusks of wild elephants which was as pale white as a piece of the *ketaki* flower. It was endowed with an iron arch that bore a string of iron mirrors with rows of red chauries that seemed to be like the faces of the Śabaras fierce with their brown hair. The pedestal of the image of Durgā was of black stone with an iron buffalo in front of it, having marks of red sandal paste made on it. The eyes of the buffalo were blood-red. Around Durgā, who was propitiated by hideous offerings, played cubs of lions which scattered about the red pearls that had been seized and then let off by foolish cocks. The door of the *garbha-gṛha* had iron spikes placed in the mouths of lions drawn in figures. The image of Durgā was dressed in red silken robes that reached below her feet and fell upon the pedestal, with a *tilaka* on her forehead, *tāmbūla* in her mouth, and *karṇapūrna* ornament in her ears. Before her was burnt incense.[63]

Temples to the goddess Caṇḍikā are scattered all over the country. We may note a few examples of rulers and citizens who were worshippers of Caṇḍikā. An inscription dated A. D. 1114 speaks of the Western Cālukya king Taila (evidently Nūrmmaḍi Tailapa, A. D. 973-997), who restored the supremacy of the Western Cālukyas after an eclipse of two hundred years by the Rāṣṭrakūṭas, as the promoter of the Cālukya kingdom and offering up the full blown the heads of his enemies at the feet of Caṇḍika.[64] Under the Hoysala Narasiṃha Deva, the *Mahāsāmanta* Uttama Coḷa ruling over the Noṇabankere Twelve and other provinces, is called "obtainer of a boon from the goddess Caṇḍikā."[65] There was an image of the same goddess in the temple of Somanātha in Mūḍukeri in Bārkūr in Tuḷuva (mod. South Kanara), to which a private person named Rāmaṇṇa, son of Hemmāḍi Joyiśa, made some provision for its worship. This is related in an inscription dated S'aka 1362 (A. D. 1440-41) found in the same Somanātha temple.[66] Goddess Caṇḍikā seems to have been praised in A. D. 1404. But the lithic record which gives us this fragmentary detail is defaced and, therefore, we cannot make out its full import.[67]

It is not only the deity of the Kirātas that has been adored but even the Kirātas themselves have been deified in Hindu literature. The celebrated episode in the *Mahābhārata* when Arjuna adopted the name, nationality, and guise of a Kirāta for a certain period, in order to learn archery and the use of other weapons from S'iva, and the rendering of this piece by Bhāravi in his immortal *Kirātārjuneya* is too well known to need a repetition here.[68]

The Kirātas have been an historical factor in the annals of our land. We have already mentioned the occasions when they appeared on the scene in the *Mahābhārata*. These following instances may also be noted. The rulers of the Daśārnas, and the Prāygas, and the Dāserakas, and the Anupakas, and the Kirātas were placed in the neck of *krauñcāruṇa* array formed by Yudhiṣṭira.[69] On the seventeenth day of the memorable battle, Kṛṣṇa told Arjuna that a great number of soldiers of terrible deeds and exceedingly fierce—the Tuṣāras, the Yavanas, the Khasas, the Dārvābhisāras, the Daradas, the S'akas, the Kamathas, the Ramathas, the Tanganas, the Andhrakas, the Pulindas, the Kirātas of fierce prowess, the Mlecchas, the mountaineers hailing from the seaside, all endowed with great wrath and might, delighting in battle and armed with maces—uniting with the Kurus and figthing wrathfully for Duryodhana's sake, were incapable of being defeated by anybody save Savyasācin.[70] On the same occasion, Sātyaki urged his charioteer to take him to that place where those Yavanas armed with bows and arrows and skilled in smiting, and the S'akas and Kirātas and Daradas and Barbaras and Tāmraliptas and other countless Mlecchas armed with diverse weapons, were stationed.[71]

Coming down to historical times, we find that Alexander the Great conquered certain wild tribes.[72] They lived on the coast near the mouth of the river Tomeros (mod. Hingol), and are described to have been a wild race of savages, ignorant of the use of iron, covering themselves with the skins of wild beasts, with claw-like nails strong enough to rip up raw fish and to split the softer kinds of wood.[73] Pliny gives one significant detail in connection with Alexander the Great and the wild tribes. The Conquerer forbade the whole of the Ichthyophagi Oritae to live any longer on raw fish.[74] Pliny describes them to be mountaineers and places them after the Gedrusi and the Pasires (in modern Dulcidan and Goadel).[75] Ptolemy, we may incidentally add, locates the Kirrhadai in Sogdiana along the Oxus.[76] We have elsewhere spoken of the Kirātas as having been mountaineers, eating raw-fish, and of having spread themselves practically over the whole of the northern part of the Indian continent. We may not be far wrong in assuming that they may have crossed the Hindu Kuṣ mountains, and occupied the banks of the Oxus, and that they may have been the wild tribes whom Alexander the Great vanquished.

The fact of their having made the Oxus basin their home in some remote period of history may explain in a measure the reason why they have been, as we have so often seen, coupled with the Yavanas and the other western peoples in the *Mahābhārata.*

The author of the well known *Mudrārākṣasa* too brings on the scene the Yavanas together with the Kirātas in a manner to indicate sufficiently the role these latter played in the history of the great Mauryan Empire. Pāṭaliputra was attacked. Virādhagupta, disguised as a snake charmer, narrates to Rākṣasa the entry of Candragupta into the palace of Nanda. The forces of Candragupta and Parvates'vara composed of S'akas, Yavanas, Kirātas, Kāmbojas, Pārasikas, Bāhlikas, and others, led by the counsels of Cāṇakya, looking like seas with waters in commotion, at the time of universal destruction, invested Kusumapura on all sides.[77]

We shall see in the next chapter that the succour which Candragupta Maurya sought of the Kirātas and the Mlecchas in attacking Pāṭaliputra, and consequently in founding his kingdom, was by no means accidental.

That the Kirātas and the kindred tribes, whose interference in Mauryan politics we have just seen above, had eastablished powerful kingdoms in the northern, north-eastern, and central parts of India by the middle of the fourth century A. D. is proved by the statements in the Allahabad Pillar inscription of Samudra Gupta. This edict which records his brilliant conquests undertaken between the years A. D. 330 and 335,[78] eulogizes the deeds of the great conqueror thus:—"Who abounded in majesty that had been increased by violently exterminating Rudradeva, Matila, Nāgadatta, Candravarman, Gaṇapatināga, Nāgasena, Acyuta, Nandi, Balvarman and many other kings of (the land of) Āryavarta;—who made all the kings of the forest countries to become (his) servants.... "[79]

The territory of these forest kings has been identified by some with the state of Orissa and the more backward parts of the Central Provinces.[80] According to others, the kingdom of Mahākāntāra of Vyāghrarāja conquered by Samudra Gupta was to the south of southern Kos'ala in the region of Jhād-Khaṇḍa (Oriya for forest country) in the Ganjam and Vizagapatam Agency tracts.[81]

But it may reasonably be doubted whether there was only one forest kingdom called Mahākāntāra ruled over by Vyāghrarāja, or many principalities of the forest tribes. The Allahabad Pillar inscription of Samudra Gupta clearly informs us that it was *all* the kings of the forest countries whom he conquered. Evidently the Vyāghrarāja mentioned herein was only one of them. We have to surmise that in the wild tracts of Central India there were other equally powerful forest chieftains whom Samudra Gupta had made his servants. About the details of his policy towards the forest rulers, we do not know anything.

But it seems certain that there were many forest kingdoms from the trend of events that took place after the reign of Samudra Gupta. The existence of eighteen forest kings in the region now made up by Bundelkand is proved by an inscription dated A. D. 528–9 of the times of the Mahārāja Saṅkṣobha recording the grant of the village of Opāṇī to the temple of the goddess Piṣṭapuri (modern Pithapuram, twenty miles north-east of Cocanada). In this inscription it is said that the Mahārāja Hastin, in whose line was born Saṅkṣobha, " sought to govern properly the kingdom of Ḍhabāla (mod. Bundelkand) which had come (to him) by inheritance together with (all the country) included in the eighteen forest kingdoms (*āṣṭādas'-āṭavi-rājya*)."[82] About these eighteen kingdoms, there is unfortunately a blank in history. It is perhaps some of these which the author of the *Bṛhatsamhitā* includes among the *vana-rāṣṭra* (forest-countries) and *vana-rājya* (forest kingdoms) in the north-east.[83]

We shall presently speak of a Niṣāda king called Pṛthvīvyāghra who had occupied a part of the territory of the Eastern Cālukya ruler Viṣṇuvardhana.

In the annals of the ancient Karṇāṭaka kingdoms of the south and the west, too, the Kirātas have figured. Thus in a record dated A. D. 713 of the Gaṅga king S'ivamāra I., the praise of Nava Kāma, the younger brother of Koṅguṇi Mahārājādhirāja Bhūvikrama, is thus sung:—" In the inner courts of the palaces of kings hostile to whom, the Kirāta women decorate their bodies with the nectar from the temples of the elephants slain by him, and see delighted the reflection of their joyous embraces in the jewelled courtyards. "[84]

The praise given to the Gaṅga king Satyavākya Koṅguṇi Vārma Dharma Mahārāja that he was " the destroyer of the groups of Kirātas dwelling on the skirts of the Vindhya forests, " as given in an inscription dated A. D. 973,[85] proves that the Kirātas continued to cause havoc in the Gaṅga kingdom, necessitating thereby the extension of the Gaṅga arms into the forests of the Vindhyas.

One of the Noḷambavāḍi rulers too vanquished the Kirātas. The following is mentioned in a record dated A. D. 943 of the Pallava king Dilīparasa:—That born in the Iśvaravaṁśa was Triṇayana, from whom was the king of Kañci, Pallava. " Born in his family, conqueror of the Kirāta king, worshipper of Caṇḍikā, was Noḷambādhirāja, praised by the Karṇāṭakas, the king named Maṅgaḷa, reverenced by the learned. "[86]

The great Tāmil king Rājarāja Deva is called

"destruction to the race of hill-chiefs" (*malepa-kuḷa-kāḷam*) in a record dated A. D. 1007.[87]

Puṇisa was the most famous general of the greatest of the Hoysala kings Viṣṇuvardhana Biṭṭi Deva. "The ruined traders, the cultivators with no seeds to sow, the ousted Kirāta (chief) with no power left, who had become his servant, he gave them all what they had lost and supported them, the *daṇḍanātha* Puṇisa"—such is the praise bestowed on him in an inscription of A. D. 1117.[88] We shall describe in detail in a subsequent chapter the measures which the Hoysala rulers took to subvert the power of the wild tribes in the Karṇāṭaka.

In the seventeenth century, too, the Kirātas gave expression to their turbulent nature. The Keladi kings, and after them, the Mysore rulers, promptly dealt with them. One example of a Keladi ruler who vanquished the Kirātas is that of Veṅkaṭapa Nāyaka. In a grant of his grandson Vīrabhadra Nāyaka dated A. D. 1641, Veṅkaṭapa Nāyaka is called "a sun to disperse the thick darkness the numberless Kirātas."[89] It will be seen that Veṅkaṭapa Nāyaka was by no means the only Keladi king who won a victory over the Kirātas.

Of the Mysore rulers Cikka Deva, grandson of Cāma Rāja IV., is said to have won many battles, and to have overcome Muṣṭika, who was supported by the Morasas (people of the Kōlār district) and the Kirātas, and to have captured Jadakanadurga re-naming it Cikka Devarāyapura. Thus does a record dated A. D. 1680 describe the conquests of one of the most celebrated monarchs of Mysore.[90]

CHAPTER III

THE S'ABARAS

Summary:— Indentity between the Kirātas and the S'abaras – Origin in the *Aitareya Brāhmaṇa* and in the *Mahābhārata* – Foreign and Hindu writers on their location – Traces in modern India – S'abara element in some of the royal families of India: the Maurya House, the Gupta family, Udayana's parentage, the Niṣāda line, the Pallava ancestry – The S'abaras in the history of southern and western India from the tenth to the seventeenth centuries – The S'abaras as a progressive factor.

According to the lexicographer Amara, there was no difference between the Kirātas, the S'abaras, the Beḍas, and the other kindred wild tribes. He classifies them under the *S'ūdravarga* thus:—

Caṇḍāla-Plava-Mātaṅga-divākir-iti-janaṅgamāḥ ।
Niṣāda-svapacāva antevāsi Cāṇḍāla Pulkasāḥ ॥
Bhedaḥ Kirāta S'abara Pulindā Mleccha-jātayaḥ ।
vyādho mṛgavadhā-jīvo mṛgayur Lubdhko-'pi saḥ ॥ [1]

This confusion between the different classes of the wild tribes was by no means confined to Amarsiṁha. Kauṭalya mentions them in the same breath in the following context:—The interior of the kingdom should be watered by trap-keepers (*vāgurika*), S'abaras, Pulindas, Caṇḍālas, and wild tribes (*araṇyacarāḥ*). [2]

With the classical lead thus given, it is not surprising that Daṇḍin in the passage we have already cited should call the S'abaras Kirātas. [3]

The *Aitareya Brāhmaṇa* has a traditional account to give of the origin of the S'abaras and other similar tribes. It says that the eldest sons of Viśvāmitra were cursed to become the progeny of the most abject races such as the Āndhras, the Puṇḍras, the Śabaras, the Pulindas, and the Mūtibas. These Dasyu tribes are said to have lived on the borders of the Āryan territory.[4]

The *Mahābhārata* elaborates this explanation thus :— Viśvāmitra forcibly had taken away the cow of Vaśiṣṭha. From her tail she began to rain showers of burning coals all round. And some moments after, from her tail she brought forth an army of Pahlavas; and from her udders, of Drāviḍas; from her womb, of Yavanas; and from her dung, of S'abaras; and from her urine, of Kāñcis; and from her sides, of S'abaras again. And from the froth of her mouth, came out hosts of Puṇḍras and Kirātas, Yavanas, and Siṅghalas, and the barbarous tribes of Khasa and Civukas and Pulindas and Cins and Huns with Keraḷas and numerous other Mlecchas. This army routed the soldiers of Viśvāmitra.[5]

The precise significance of this legend is still a matter of uncertainty. We, therefore, pass on to the topic of the location of the Śabaras as recorded by foreign writers and in Hindu literature. According to Megasthenes, towards the Indus were a number of people. Immediately beyond came deserts extending for 250 miles. Those being crossed, one came to the Organagae, Abaortae, Sibarae, Sauertae and after these came deserts again as extensive as the former.[6]

Next to the Prasii, in the interior, Pliny writes, came the Monedes and the Suari to whom belonged Mount Maleus on which shadows fell towards the north in winter , and to the south in summer, for six months alternately.[7]

Towards the Ganges were the Sabarai in whose country diamond was found in great abundance. Thus informs Ptolemy,[8] who noted one particular class of the S'abaras whom he called the Phyllitac. Fleet, as we shall presently narrate, wrongly identified them with leaf-*eating* S'abaras.

The S'abaras, therefore, had moved eastwards from somewhere near the Indus in the times of Megasthenes to the Gangetic basin in the age of Ptolemy. That is to say, they had made the Madhya-des'a their home.

The Hindu writers confirm the accounts of the foreign geographers in this detail. The Deccan and Central India are mentioned in the *Rāmāyaṇa* as being the regions occupied by the wicked Dasyus called the S'abaras who were given over to the practice of evil customs.[9] But the same epic mentions a pious S'abara figure. It is that of the S'ramaṇa S'abari who had a hermitage on the western side of the Paṁpā lake (in the neighbourhood of modern Haṁpe). Not far om it arrived Rāma and reached her dwelling. Before her time the hermitage had been occupied by the Ṛṣi Mātaṅga.[10]

The *Bṛhatsaṃhitā* has some notices of the S'abaras confirming, on the whole, the statements in the *Rāmāyaṇa* that they were found in the southern regions and in central India. The western and south-eastern homes of the S'abaras and the Niṣādas, together with the habitat of a particular branch of the S'abaras called the Nagna-Parṇa-S'abaras, are thus given in the *Bṛhatsaṃhitā*:—

> Vṛṣanālikeracarmadvipā Vindhyānta-vāsinaḥ-tripurī I
> s'mas'radhara Hemakūṭya Vyālagrivā Mahāgrīvāḥ II
> Kiṣkindha-kaṇṭhakasthala Niṣāda-rāṣṭrāṇi purikā Dās'ārṇāḥ I
> saha Nagna-parṇa-S'abaraih-ās'leṣādhyaitrike des'āḥ II [11]

The author of the same work, however, couples them with the Vaṅgas, the Suhmas, the Kaliṅgas, the Bāhlikas, the S'akas, the Yavanas, the Maghadas, and the people of Prāgjyotiśa, Cīna, and Kāmboja.[12] In another connection he speaks of the S'abaras, the Ābhiras, the Pahlavas, the Mallas, the Matsyas, and the S'akas all together.[13]

The Nagna-Parṇa-S'abaras mentioned above were not, as Kern and Fleet interpreted,[14] naked leaf-eating S'abaras but leaf-wearing S'abaras, as Gerini rightly pointed out.[15]

The *Mārkaṇḍeya Purāṇa* locates the Parṇa-S'abaras among the people who lived in the right fore-foot (of the Tortoise).[16] The S'abaras are also mentioned along with the Pulindas in the same work as living in the southern regions.[17]

The *Matsya Purāṇa* includes among the *dakṣiṇā-patha-janapadas* (southern countries) those of the Aiṣīkas, the Āṭaviyas, the S'abaras, the Pulindas, and the rest.[18]

These tribes too have left vestiges behind them in the history of the land. The Suari of Pliny and the S'abarae of Ptolemy were indentified by Cunningham with the S'abaras or Suars, a wild race of cultivators who live in the jungles without any inhabitation.[19] They may be said in general to have occupied the central parts of India. But they have left their relics in other provinces as well. Cunningham identified the famous place of pilgrimage, S'avari Nārāyaṇ, lying on the high road from Bilāspur to Jagannāth,- about thirty-five miles to the south-west of Bilāspur and seventy-five miles north-east of Rāypur,- with the chief town of the S'abaras (the Sorae Nomades of the foreign writers) called *Sora Arcati regia*. The people of the locality refer the name S'avari Nārāyaṇ to the S'rmaṇa S'avarı of the *Rāmāyaṇa* mentioned above. The oldest building existing at S'avari Nārāyaṇ is the temple of the Sun (*arka*), and this was probably what the foreigners referred to when they spoke of the *Arcati regia.* That the temple now holds a figure of Viṣṇu is no justification for supposing that it was a Vaiṣṇavite temple. The existence of an original dedication to the Sun god is proved by the figure of the god being placed over the middle of the doorway.[20]

Another place which Cunningham identified with the S'abaras is the ruined site near Ghāzipur. This is still called Suirkaraj. It is said to have received its name from the Süirs or S'avaras, which recalls at once the S'avari Nārāyaṇ on the Mahānadī.[21]

Sambhalpur which produced the finest diamonds in the world, is also thought by some to have been once inhabited by the S'abaras. In fact, their presence today in this area proves our contention.[22]

To the south-west of Gwalior and Narwar and South Rajputana are a race known as the Surris. They were the Saurs or the S'abaras.[23]

Under the name of S'abar, Saur, Süirs, S'avarulu, etc., they inhabit the wild tracts of Damoh, Saugor, Singhbhum, Orissa, Chota Nagpur, the Ganjam and Vizagapatam districts. They are today a wild nomadic race, wandering over the hills, living on the fruits of the forests, and acknowledging the rule of no recognized chief.[24]

The most powerful of these wild races in the early centuries of the Christian era, according to the opinion of Cunningham, were the Parṇa-S'abaras. He conjectured that the chief town in the country of the Phyllitae (*i. e.,* the Parṇa-S'abaras or the leaf-wearing

S'abaras) and of the *Kondali*, called Agara, was probably Sagar.[25] These Parṇa-S'abaras have been identified with the Pāṇs, a very low aboriginal caste in Orissa and the Eastern Circars.[26] The term Parṇa-S'abara (leaf-wearing S'abara) may appropriately be applied to the women in the wilder parts of the Cānda district of the Central Provinces, who wear no clothes at all but only a string round the waist to which they suspend a bunch of leaves and another behind. The same practice is reported to exist in the Kōl country and also in Orissa.[27]

To these leaf-wearing classes of Śabaras we may add those of South Kanara who are called the Soppu (Toppu) Koragars. These are one class of the aboriginal people who wear leaves round their waist. The larger tribe to which they belong played an important part in the early history of the district.*

With the above notices of the S'abaras, we may dispense with the erroneous notions of Rice that the modern Sāukārs (traders) were S'abara in origin, and that the latter belonged to a race who worshipped the moon.[28]

We have admirable sketches of the S'abaras from the pen of Bāṇa. He describes the S'abaras who lived in the forests of the Vindhyas. They killed the lions for the pearls attached to their nails.[29]

The parrot Vais'ampāyana describes how it saw the S'abara army in the Vindhyan forests, in the same work thus :—

The S'abara army came from the wood like the strength of the Narmadā tossed by Arjuna's thousand arms; like a wood of *tamālas* stirred by the wind; like all the nights of the dark fortnight rolled into one;

* See the writer's work on *Early Tuḷuva*.

like a solid pillar of antimony shaken by an earthquake; like a grave darkness disturbed by sunbeams; like the followers of Death roaming; like the demon world that had burst open hell and risen up; like a crowd of evil deeds come together; like a caravan of curses of the many hermits dwelling in the Daṇḍaka forest; like all the hosts of Dūṣaṇa and Khara struck by Rāma as he raised his ceaseless shafts, and they turned into demons, for their hatred to him; like the whole confraternity of the Iron Age come together; like a band of buffaloes prepared for a plunge into the water; like a mass of black clouds broken by a blow from the lion's paw as he stands on the mountain peak; like a throng of meteors risen for the destruction of all form; it darkened the wood; it numbered many thousands; it inspired great dread; it was like a multitude of demons portending disasters.[30]

We may be permitted to continue the description of the S'abara commander whom Vaiśampāyana saw in the midst that great host of the S'abaras. The name of the Śabara leader was Mātaṅga. He was yet in early youth. From his great hardness he seemed to be made of iron. He was like Ēkalavya (the king of the Niṣādas killed by Kṛṣṇa, as related in the Mahābhārata,)[31] in another birth. From his growing beard, he was like a young royal elephant with its temple encircled by its first line of ichor. He filled the wood with beauty that streamed from him sombre as dark lotuses, like the waters of the Yamunā. He had thick locks curled at the ends and hanging on his shoulders like a lion with its mane stained by elephant's ichor. His brow was broad, his nose was stern and acquiline; his left side shone reddened by the faint pink rays of a jewelled snake's hood that was made the ornament for one of his ears, like the glow of shoots that had clung to him from his resting on a leafy couch. He was perfumed with fragrant ichor, bearing the scent of *saptaccheda* blossoms torn from the cheeks of an elephant freshly slain, like a stain of black aloes. He had the heat warded off by a swarm of bees, like a peacock feather parasol flying about blinded by the scent, as if they were a branch of *tamāla.* He was marked with lines of perspiration on his cheek rubbed by his hand, as if Vindhya forest, being conquered by his strong arm, were timidly offering homage under the guise of its slender waving twigs; and he seemed to tinge space by his eyes somewhat pink, as if it were bloodshot, and shedding a twilight of the night of doom for the deer. He had mighty arms reaching to his knees, as if the measure of an elephant's trunk had been taken in making them; and his shoulders were rough with scars from keen weapons often used to make an offering to Kālī. The space round his eyes was bright and broad as the Vindhya mountains, and with the drops of dried deer's blood clinging on it, and the marking of drops from an elephant's frontal bone mixed with the *guñja* fruit. His chest was scarred by constant and ceaseless fatigue.

He was clad in a silk dress red with cochineal; and with his strong legs he mocked a pair of elephants' posts stained with elephants' ichor. He seemed from his causeless fierceness to have marked on his broad brow by a frown that formed three banners, as if Durgā, propitiated by his great devotion, had marked him with a trident to denote that he was her servant.

He was accompanied by hounds of every colour, which were his familiar friends; they showed their weariness by the tongues that, dry as they were, seemed by their natural pinkness to drip deer's blood, and which hung down from tiredness; as their mouths were open they raised the corners of their lips and showed their flashing teeth clearly, like a lion's mane caught between the teeth; their throats were covered with strings of couries, and they were hacked by blows from the large boar's tusks. Though but small, from their great strength they were like lion's cubs with their manes ungrown. They were skilled in initiating the does in widowhood; with them came their wives, very large, like lionesses coming to beg an amnesty for the lions.

The S'abara leader was surrounded by troops of S'abaras of all kinds: some had seized elephants' tusks and the long hair of yāks; some had vessels for honey made of leaves closely bound; some, like lions, had hands filled with many a pearl from the frontal bones of elephants; some, like demons, had pieces of raw flesh; some, like goblins, were carrying the skins of lions; some, like Jaina ascetics, held peacocks', tails; some, like children, wore crows' feathers; some represented Kṛṣṇa's exploits by bearing the elephants' tusks they had torn out; some, like the days of the rainy season, had garments dark as clouds. [32]

That the description of the S'abara commander may be complete, we give the following details found in the same work. The S'abara leader had his sword in sheath, as a wood its rhinoceres; like a fresh cloud, he held a bow bright as peacock's tails; like the demon Baka he possessed a peerless army; like Garuḍa, he had torn out the teeth of many large nāgas; he was hostile to peacocks as Bhīṣma to S'iknaṇḍi...as the locks of Umā were decked with S'iva's moon, so was he adored with the eyes of peacock's tails; as the demon

Hiraṇyakas ipu by Mahāvarāha, so he had his breast torn by the teeth of a great boar; like an ambitious man, he had a train of captives around him; like a demon, he loved the hunters; like the gamut of a song, he was closed in by Niṣādas; like the trident of Durgā, he was wet with the blood of buffaloes.[33]

With the above magnificent description before us the following may seem to be a meagre sketch of the S'abaras given by a Kannaḍa poet. Nevertheless, in order to acquaint ourselves with a portraiture from the south, we may note what Braham-kavi (circa A. D. 1600) has to say concerning the S'abara women:—

With black bodies, wearing the sprouts of *as'oka* plant, and the (beautiful scarlet and black) seeds of the wild liquorice (*guru-guñji*) and the black pearls obtained from the bamboos in their braids, the S'abara women shone like *sandhyā*-Lakṣmī (or twilight):—

Kariyaru kāyada as'oke–taḷiram-uṭṭu guru-guñji sara koraloḷago ।
kari vēṇu mutta muḍige kaṭṭi sañjeya siriya-ante-iharu
S'abariyaru ॥[34]

The religious beliefs of the S'abaras were much the same as those of the Kirātas and other kindred tribes. They were, as we have already seen, worshippers of the goddess Caṇḍikā or Durgā. The following account of the faith common among the S'abaras of the Telugu districts called the Koṇḍa S'avaralu and the Malijala S'avarulu, may be read in conjunction with the remarks we have already noted from Daṇḍin's *Das'akumāracarita* regarding the sacrifice of a fair child to the goddess Caṇḍikā. The Koṇḍa S'avarulu and the Malijala S'avarulu hold a festival called Toki. About forty to fifty villages take part in it, selecting one village by turn for the site of the operation. It is held in honour of Jāgrata Deva, a local deity. Four or five months before the time fixed for the festival, the most important item is made, *viz.*, the selection of some friendless man of the age of twenty or twenty-six years, as an offering to the deity. The person is seized, put into confinement, highly fed and allowed the free use of intoxicants. For eight or nine successive days at the time of the sacrifice, the victim is taken in public procession round the village where the sacrifice is to be held. The precise act is at 4 o'clock in the morning, or an hour or two before sunrise. The victim is killed by a weapon called *gaṇḍa-goḍali;* and the blood is used as offering to the deity. Nothing is known of the eating of the flesh of the victim.[35]

How far the S'abaras have influenced Indian history needs now to be examined. Their aid was called into requisition in the troublesome times of the foundation of the Mauryan Empire. Viśākhadatta in his well known drama already referred to, informs us that Rākṣasa, on his way to Prince Malayaketu (who had summoned him on hearing the alleged plot), told Priyamvadaka, thus:—" Let the chiefs that follow the Prince be informed in my name that they should proceed *en route* in the proposed order, now that they are nearer and nearer to Kusumapura every day–Khasa and S'abara chiefs should march in the van in battle array after me. Yavana chiefs should be careful to keep the centre along with Gāndhāra chiefs. Valiant S'aka chiefs accompanied by Hūṇa chiefs should be in the rear. And the remaining group of chiefs, namely the king of Kulūta, etc. should post themselves about the person of Prince Malayaketu in the line of march."[36]

The fact of the foreign or Mleccha kings having helped either side during the eventful days of the establishment of the Mauryan kingdom being thus proved beyond doubt, the question arises-How do we account for the presence of the foreign powers, especially of the forces of the Kirātas and the S'abaras, whom Candragupta enlisted in his service during the investment of Pāṭaliputra ? On a closer analysis of the question, one is inclined to think that the assistance which the wild tribes gave to Candragupta Maurya was not merely adventitious. There may have been, we venture to say, an identity of interests between the future Emperor of Āryavarta and the most powerful of the Mleccha tribes. This may have been in regard to their common origin. Candragupta is acknowledged to have been a Kṣatriya. The *Mahāvamso*, for instance, narrates that, after the nine Nandas, the Brāhmaṇ Cāṇakka annointed a glorious youth, known by the name of Candagutta, as king over all Jambudīpa, born of a noble clan the Moriyas, when filled with bitter hate, he had slain the ninth Dhanananda.[37] Other evidence, which we abstain from recording, is also overwhelmingly in favour of Candragupta being considered a Kṣatriya.

But on the strength of the assertions of Viśākhadatta and those of Manu confirmed by the statements in the *Mahābhārata*, it is permissible to ask whether or not there was a distinct S'abara element in the parentage of Candragupta. Cāṇakya calls him in the drama mentioned above, as is too well known, by the name Vṛśāla Maurya.[38] The term *Vṛs'āla* seems to have had some particular significance in the code of lawgivers. Under that denomination were included a number of wild tribes, as we had an occasion of explaining on the evidence of the *Mahābhārata* and the *Code of Manu*, among whom were the Kirātas and the S'abaras.

The name Vṛśāla, it may also be noted, carried with it a certain amount of what we may be permitted to call un-Aryanism which is thus explained by the legists. The *Bṛhadāraṇyaka Upaniṣad* says the following:— "When the monthly illness seizes his wife, she should for three days not drink from a metal vessel, and wear a fresh dress. Let no Vṛśāla or Vṛśālī touch her."[39] A Snātaka was forbidden to go alone on a journey with outcastes or with a woman or with a S'ūdra who was evidently no other than a Vṛs'ūla.[40] Manu pronounced the following verdict on those who dared to violate justice:—"For divine justice (is said to be) a bull (vṛṣa); that (man) who violates it (*kurute'lam*) the gods consider to be (a man despicable like) a S'ūdra (Vṛs'āla); let him, therefore, beware of violating justice."[41]

The pointed reference which Cāṇakya often makes to the Vṛs'āla parentage of Candragupta Maurya and the substantial aid which the latter received from the S'abaras and the Kirātas, who appear frequently on the scene in the drama *Mudrārākṣasa*, suggest that Candragupta, notwithstanding the most substantial claims he had for being considered a true Kṣatriya by virtue of his remarkable military achievements,—in the wider sense of the term—, may have been of S'abara or Kirāta (*i. e.*, S'ūdra) stock not only from his mother's side, as is admitted, but also from his paternal line, about which, however, it must be confessed, direct evidence is not forthcoming in history. The indomitable courage which characterized the achievements of Candragupta could not have been native to a S'ūdra, however well trained he may have been in the use of arms. And the wise Brāhmaṇ counsellor would not have selected as a tool a man from the ordinary ranks had he not been certain of the sterner and wilder nature of the origin from which Candragupta had sprung.

Turning to another royal family, we find that in regard to that too, we have some valid grounds for tracing its lineage to the wild tribes. We refer to the Gupta royal house. The *Viṣṇu Purāṇa* has classed the Guptas with the Vaiśyas and the S'ūdras: while the termination *s'arman* is prescribed for a Brāhmaṇa, *varman* belongs to a Kṣatriya, and a name characterized by Gupta or Dāsa is approved of in the case (respectively) of a Vaiśya and a S'ūdra.[42]

This definition of the names Gupta and Dāsa is not without classical sanction. In the *Mahābhārata* the Dāsas are classified among the *anuloma* and *pratiloma* castes. From the Niṣādas, the epic informs us, sprang a caste called Madgura and another named Dāsa whose occupation consisted in plying boats.[43] The explanation given herein may be traced to Manu, who lays it down that a Kaivarta or Dāsa, or, also as he was called, Mārgava, was an offspring of a Niṣāda by an Āyogava woman, his occupation being that of a boatman.[44]

The origin of these Dāsas or Kaivartas being thus traced by the classical canonists to the Niṣāda stock, it remains to be seen which of the royal families of India could be referred to a similar consanguinity. The Guptas as well as a later family connected in some manner with them, may be cited as examples of royal houses which had their origin in stock outside the pale of the *varṇās'ramas*. It may be argued that Candra Gupta I married a Licchavi princess,[45] and that, therefore, he was a Kṣatriya monarch. But the following considerations not only demolish the claims that may be put forward to prove his Kṣatriya origin but also lend support to the view that he was of a stock allied to that of the S'abaras and other wild tribes. In the praise bestowed on Samudra Gupta in the Allahabad Pillar inscription no mention whatsoever is made of the Kṣatriya descent either of that ruler or of any of his predecessors. This itself clearly demonstrates that the people did not associate the early Guptas with the Kṣatriyas. Turning to the Licchavi alliance of Candra Gupta, it may be said that the Licchavis, inspite of their having been eulogized in Buddhist literature as a Kṣatriya clan, were in the opinion of Manu, Sūdras.[46] The prominence given to the marriage of the Licchavi princess Kumāra Devī with Candra Gupta as narrated in the inscriptions and coins, may be interpreted to mean, not that Candra Gupta was a Kṣatriya, but that his alliance transformed his house into a family that had great pretensions to celebrity.

Evidence from another quarter may be utilized in order to show that the early Guptas belonged to a family that was outside the pale of the orthodox *varṇā-s'ramas*. If the identification of Caṇḍa Sena mentioned in the drama *Kaumudīmahotsava* with Candra Gupta is accepted, then the statement made in that drama that he was a Kāraskara only confirms our surmise concerning the low origin of the Guptas. For the Kāraskaras, according to Baudhāyana, were a low community to whom Brāhmaṇs ought not to go, and on return from whom they should perform purificatory ceremonies.[47] The feeling of repugnance with which Baudhāyana condemns the Kāraskaras is almost the same sense of aloofness which the other canonists associated with the Śabaras, the Kirātas, and the rest. It must be confessed, however, that an identity either of origin or interests between the Kāraskaras and the wild tribes under review cannot be made for the present.[48]

A further proof of the non-Kṣatriya origin, if one may say so, of the Guptas is afforded in the epigraphs relating to the lineage of the Kośala rulers. These may be said to have been connected with the earlier Guptas. The Kośala rulers were lords of Magadha. The Rajim copper-plate inscription of the Mahās'iva Tīvararāja informs us that Tīvara Deva was the adopted son of Nanna Deva whose grand-father was Udayana of the Śavara lineage.[49]

Udayana's date may be fixed in the following manner : His activities extended as far as the Tamil land. He is said to have been conquered, captured, and released again by the later Pallava king Nandivarman. The exact date of this Pallava monarch is uncertain. His general Udaya Candra is said to have slain Udayana, and to have seized his mirror-banner embellished with peacock's tail.[50] Now the same Pallava general Udaya Candra is credited with a victory over the Nis'āda king Pṛthvīvyāghra, who was performing an *as'vamedha* sacrifice, and who had occupied a part of the territory of the Eastern Cālukya king Viṣṇuvardhana (A. D. 709-746). Pṛthvīvyāghra was driven out of the territory of Viṣṇu-rāja (*i.e.*, Viṣṇuvardhana). If this victory of Udaya Candra over Pṛthvīvyāghra can be credited, Udayana may be placed in the later half of the eighth century A. D., thereby justifying Fleet's conjectures.[51]

Before we proceed to deal with the Pallavas, we may note that the Kaivartas who, as has been just remarked above, are classed with the Dāsas in the writings of the Hindu canonists, played a significant part in the history of Bengal and Tuḷuva. Divya or

Divyoka was the powerful chief of the Cāsi-Kaivarta tribe (mod. Kervat caste) in northern Bengal. He rebelled against king Mahīpāla (II) in about A. D. 1080. Ballāl Sen, we may add, is said to have conquered northern Bengal with the help of the Kaivartas, and to have attempted at giving them a higher social status. In the history of eastern Bengal too the Kaivartas have figured.[52] Tradition relates that in distant Tuḷuva from among the Kaivartas Paras'urāma recruited Brāhmaṇs to colonize the land he had reclaimed from the sea.

The Pallavas themselves seem to have had some S'abara blood in their veins, at least according to tradition. We confess that the story of their origin is another riddle that awaits solution. But we may note that Mukunti Pallava, supposed by some to have been the founder of the Pallava line with his capital at Dharaṇikoṭa, is said to have been a son of Mahādeva (S'iva) by a girl of the wild mountain tribe called the Censuaras (*i.e.*, the Cen-S'abaras).[53] These Censuaras were no doubt the same as the modern Cencu, Cenju, or Irala tribes found in the Goomsoor wilds, and westward of Ahobalam, S'rīs'ailam, as well as in the North and South Arcot districts. They are also called Villiyans or bowmen. The males put on skins, and women, stitched leaves. They live on the rice of the bamboo. They are also found near Pulicat, twenty-four miles north of Madras along the sea, under the name of Centsus.[54]

The Karṇāṭaka was a region which suffered most from the depradations of the wild tribes. Of these only the S'abaras concern us here. In the reign of the Gaṅga king Satyavākya Permmānaḍi, as is related in a record dated A. D. 972, the Brāhmaṇs of Tagare-nāḍ went on a mission to Mārasiṅgha Permmānaḍi. He was a great soldier, as his *birudu Noḷambakulāntaka*, among others, clearly testifies. It is possible that he ruled over Gaṅgavāḍi Nine-Thousand (?). The occasion was a grave one :— a S'abara leader called Naraga was slaying and laying waste with fire all the country round. And the Brāhmaṇs approached Mārasiṅgha Permmānaḍi with the petition :— "We have come to make known (our wants). " The great soldier replied :— "I will in future (myself) rule over cows and Brāhmaṇs, the war-army and the treasury, the foot-soldiers and over Naraga : I grant your petition. " Forthwith at his command, his soldiers slew Naraga together with his son-in-law, his childern, his family, subjects and slaves. But Mārasiṅgha's soldiers died nobly in the struggle.[55]

It is not surprising that the cruel perpetrations of the wild tribes about this time (the tenth century A. D.) should have been echoed in the writings of contemporary Kannaḍa writers. Abhinava Paṁpā, who has already appeared in these pages, has many interesting details to give of the havoc which the S'abaras caused to the people. He calls the S'abara leader Taraṅgatama, king of the great Mleccha-deśa, with his capital at Ardhapura, north of Dhanadacala and south of Vijayārdhacala. His encampment (*s'ibira*) was Mayūramale. He plundered in every direction the territory of king Janaka including Kapōta, Kāmbōja, etc., and caused such great havoc that the king had at last to seek the aid of Rāma and Lakṣmaṇa. In the battle the S'abara leader was of course defeated.[56]

There seems to have been a S'abara principality even in the times of the Vijayanagara monarch Sāḷuva Nṛsiṁha. This we gather from Rājanātha Ḍinḍima's

Sāḷuvābhyudayam which narrates that at the request of a people called Kuṭavacalendrataṭavāsi, Sāḷūva Nṛsiṁha invaded Nāgamaṅgala. Leaving a garrison there, he proceeded to conquer Pṛthugiri. Here he was attacked by a S'abara leader. Dr. S. Krishnaswami Aiyangar incorrectly asserted that " At that place (*i. e.*, Pṛthugiri, which Dr. Aiyangar identified with Penugoṇḍa) he was attacked by a Muhammadan army. " Rājanātha, however, clearly says the following:-

Tatra (*Pṛthugirim* ?) *nṛpatiḥ-avalokitavān Cchabaraṃ tṛṇīkritajagat-trayaṃ balāt.*[57]

From this it may safely be deduced that the *Cchabara* mentioned herein could only have been a S'abara leader. It is only in the next verse that Rājanātha speaks of the Turuṣkas (Canto VI. v. 13). An examination of the route taken by Sāḷuva Nṛsiṃha as described in Canto VI of the same work will convince us that Dr. Aiyangar's identification is altogether untenable. Even supposing that we accept his identification of Nāgamaṅgala with Nāgamaṇḍala, we cannot conceive of the Vijayanagara ruler fighting now at Nāgamaṅgala and then being suddenly present at Penukoṇḍa–which is identified with Pṛthugiri–without mention being made of the regions lying between these two distant centres. Apart from this difficulty of the distance between Nāgamaṅgala and Penukoṇḍa, there is another consideration which demolishes Dr. Aiyangar's guess concerning Penukoṇḍa. Penukoṇḍa was called Suragiri and not Pṛthugiri.[57a] Further, the fact that Sāḷuva Nṛsiṃha subjugated another Dasyu king–the ruler of Das'ārṇa,–as we shall mention later on, clearly proves that he was still in the hilly tracts of the Karṇāṭaka.

It may legitimately be supposed that the S'abara

leader whom Sāḷuva Nṛsiṃha conquered was one of the Dasyu chiefs nearabouts Candragutti. We know that this region was held by the Dasyu Nāyakas from Keladi Basava Rāja's *S'ivatattvaratnākara.*[57b] The only consideration that may be brought against this identification is that *S'ivatattvaratnākara* being a work of a later age, its author may not have been well informed of the exact nature of the chiefs who held the region round about Candragutti. As against this it may be argued that the Keladi rulers, as will be described at once, were too well acquainted with the forest tribes to mistake them for other people, and that, therefore, Keladi Basava Rāja's assertion concerning the Dasyu chiefs may be given credence.

In the previous pages we observed the activities of Veṅkaṭapa Nāyaka of Keladi and how he broke the power of the Kirātas. The tradition of vanquishing the wild tribes was handed over to him by his grandfather Sadās'iva Rāya Nāyaka, son of Cauḍapa Bhadrapa. The *Keladi Nṛpati Vijaya* narrates that once Kṛṣṇa Deva Rāya heard that the S'abaras were causing great havoc in his Empire. He summoned Sadās'iva Rāya Nāyaka, ordered an efficient army to be got ready, and commanded him to destroy the enemies, having honoured him with the *tāmbūlam* (*i. e.*, betel leaf and nut). In the encounter the royal troops were at first worsted and driven back. Then the Keladi chief meditating on the god of Srī-Rudres'vara, quickly mounted on a horse, pierced the ranks of the enemy, and defeated them.[58]

The S'abaras certainly were agents of turmoil. But they were not so barbarous as not to come within the civilizing influence around them. In the age of the epics itself, a certain amount of dignity seems to have been attached to the name S'abara. This may perhaps explain why in the *Mahābhārata* Bhava assumes the form of Brahmā and Viṣṇu and the chief of the celestials. He also assumes the forms of men and women, of Pretas and Pis'ācas, of Kirātas and S'abaras, and of aquetic animals.[59]

In the *Pampā Rāmāyaṇa* we have Rudra disguising himself as a S'abara, and accompanied by Pārvatī, Guha, and others, pursuing Mūkadānava, who had assumed the form of a boar.[60] The same work relates in an *upakathe* of Vasubhūti being born as a S'abara under the name of Kālajaṅgha in the S'ārdūlasya forest.[61] A S'abara messenger is introduced in the same work as hurrying with a report that a large elephant had broken loose in the royal garden of king Janaka.[62]

The turbulent S'abara leader who caused great havoc to the Brāhmaṇs of Tagare-nāḍ, as reported in an epigraph dated A. D. 972 already cited, was a S'abara minister (*Śabara Pradhāna*), as his *birudu* signifies. His other titles were *Narakāsura* and *A most formidable opponent equal to Kāla and Śiśupāla.*[63]

The history of the *agrahāra* Beḷḷūr *alias* Viṣṇuvardhana-caturvedimaṅgalam, contains some pleasant notices of S'abaras who came within the pale of civilization. The epigraph which gives us this information relates that several S'rīvaiṣṇava scholars in that *agrahāra* village had a large number of disciples both among Brāhmaṇs and non-Brāhmaṇs. A few of their descendants, we may observe by the way, still live in that village. One of the leaders of this village was *Prativādi-bhayaṅkaram (A Terror to hostile Disputants*) Aṇṇa, a disciple of Maṇavāḷamahāmuni, the great S'rīvaiṣṇava teacher and author who flourished in the fourteenth and fifteenth centuries. One of the ancestors of the villagers then living, named Veḷḷūrappa or Annaṅgarācārya, came from Kāñci and settled in that village some 120 years ago. On hearing that some of his S'abara disciples were addicted to beef, he became disgusted and made up his mind to leave the place for Melkoṭe. Thereupon the S'abaras swore on his foot-prints that they would give up their wild habits, and entreated him to remain. The foot-prints are still pointed out on a rock on the Cikka-Urukala Guḍḍa to the west under the name *Gurugaḷa-pāda* (the Guru's feet).[64]

It is not improbable that the S'abaras, like the other mountain tribes, have ever been proficient in occult arts. To the highly cultured Jaina mind, their occult art was a wrong science. We gather this from the *Jaina Sūtras* which, while explaining the subject of man's success by occult sciences, declare that some men, differing in intellect, will, character, opinions, taste, undertakings, and places, study various evil sciences, as for example, the art of casting people asleep, of opening doors, of Cāṇḍalas, S'abaras, Draviḍas, Kaliṅgas, etc. These and similar sciences are practised by some misguided people for the sake of food, drink, clothes, a bed, and various objects of pleasure.[65]

CHAPTER IV

THE BEDARS

Summary :—Location—Modern traces—Description—The Beḍars as disintegrating factors from the seventh to the end of the eighteenth centuries A. D.—The Beḍars as progressive people : in the Hindu armies, as kingdom builders, and as contributors to Hindu thought and culture.

Of greater prominence than either the S'abaras or the Kirātas, at least so far as the history of southern and western India is concerned, were the Beḍars. These wild tribes, however, were not confined only to the western and southern parts of India. In their more northern settlements they were known by the name of Ramosi, whom they resembled in many particulars.[1] They are also met with in the traditions of the Sutlej valley. Once in twelve years a great fair is held in Outer Sarāj Nirmand in the Nūrpur valley on the Sutlej, in the temple of Devī Amba (Ambakkā ? Aṁbikā ?). Tradition relates that Paras'urāma, in expiation for the sin of having killed his mother, gave lands to the Brāhmaṇs of Nirmand, who in return agreed to spend one-tenth of the produce of this Bhunda fair. As the Beḍa caste was appointed to ride down the rope, the fair was called Bhunda, though some say that Bhunda is a corruption of *bhaṇḍāra* or temple treasury.[2]

In the history of the southern and western provinces of India the term Beḍa, or Beḍar, or Vedar has meant everything low and vile. The Beḍars were considered as outcastes, or Cāṇḍālas, living by chase. Tradition in Mysore says that they came originally from Telingāna (the Telugu country[3]), although history has a different opinion to give on this question.

The whole of the Karṇāṭaka, the Toṇḍaimaṇḍalam, Wynād (the ancient Bayalnāḍ, in the Malabar district), and the North and South Arcot districts may be said to be the regions which suffered most from the Beḍar incursions. We shall relate presently what they did in the Karṇāṭaka in regard to these wild tribes. We shall first turn our attention to their activities in the Tamil and Telugu lands. Our source of information for this part of the question is tradition. After the deluge, so runs the Tamil tradition of the Toṇḍaimaṇdalam, the country was a vast forest, inhabited by wild beasts and savage men. These were the Vedars. They lived in huts and were not at all civilized. They were conquered by the Kurumbars who came from the Karṇaṭaka.[4]

Similar tradition peoples the Wynād tracts with the wild and naked savages called the Vedars in early times after the flood. In later ages the chieftains of the locality, perceiving them to be free from guile, took them into their service. The Vedars ultimately built for themselves a fort in the Wynād country and ruled over a small tract till the Malayalam kings absorbed them in the Keraḷa kingdoms.[5]

They also occupied, tradition narrates, the North and South Arcot districts somewhere in the second century of the Christian era.[6] Evidently Arcot, as its name signifies, was an ideal habitat for the Beḍars (Āṛu-kāḍu = Six Forests).

Here in Arcot the Vedars were conquered by the

Kurumbars. Tradition, therefore, connects the Vedars with the Kurumbars, and especially with Ādoṇḍai Cakravarti, son of Kulottuṅga Coḷa Deva.[7] Whether the Kurumbars were a more cultured race than the Beḍars, or whether they belonged to the same stock as the latter, cannot be made out. The Toṇḍaimaṇḍalam tradition referred to above, informs us that the Kurumbars had a certain kind of religion but were murderers, and that they derived their name from their cruelty.[8] We have explained elsewhere in detail the role these Kurumbars played together with the barbers and the Vaṇṇiyars and other tribes in the history of the Empire of Vijayanagara in the sixteenth century.[9] If we accept the tradition that the Kurumbars drove the Beḍars (and occupied the centres of the latter), then, we may have some idea of the settlements of the two tribes in the early ages of Tamil and Karṇāṭaka history.

Some of their strongholds in the North Arcot district were Melpāḍu, sixteen miles south-west of Chittoor; the hamlet of Kōṭanattam; Paḍaveḍu, ten miles north of Polur and eighteen miles south of Vellore; Nārāyaṇavanam, three miles east of Puttoor railway station; Tiruvadis'ūlam to the east of Chingleput; and Mahendravāḍi, ten miles east by north of Wālājapet.[10]

The Kurumbars of the Palmaner plateau are reckoned to be the lineal descendants of the old Dravidian lords of the soil.[11] Ādoṇḍai Cakravarti mentioned above, is said to have subverted their chief citadel of Puralūr (mod. Poṟal *alias* Mādhavaram, near the Red Hills in the vicinity of Madras); and with it the whole territory of the Kurumbars comprising twenty-four *nāḍs* (or districts), among which those described above are to be included, passed into the hands of the Coḷā ruler. These Coḷa annexations are placed in the eleventh century of the Christian era.[12]

Other places which the wild tribes had made their home were the Ānamalai (Elephant Hills) of the Dārāpuram district and the Dindigul Hills.[13] The tribes inhabiting these latter mountains are called the Kattata *jāti* and the Kongala *jāti*. They live near Kollan-Koṭai and Kannapaṭṭi.[14]

Whether the robber and criminal classes called still the Kaḷḷars are to be included among the general denomination of the wild tribes is a point which cannot be satisfactorily solved for the present. It is possible that the socially excommunicated or politically ostracized sections of the cultured classes may have formed these robber clans and that they may have taken to the precarious livelihood of highwaymen. It may as well be that they formed a community by themselves.[15]

The Telugu land, as the reader must have gathered from the remarks made in connection with the S'abara origin of the Pallavas, likewise contained settlements of the wild tribes, some of whom, as their name signifies, seem to have been akin to the S'abaras. These were the Cencuvandlu, Coyavandlu, Yānādulu, and the Iraluvandlu. The traditional account of the Yānādu *jāti* of the S'rīharikoṭṭa tracts relates that about sixty families of their people colonized S'rīharikoṭṭa under the leadership of Rāghava.

These wild tribes were, as they are, reputed to be skilful in the use of black art, the Yānādulu being also credited with a certain amount of the knowledge of medicine. An instance of the magical skill of the Coya people may be given. It is said to have taken place in the S'aka year 1635 (A. D. 1713-14) in the woods to the north of Palavam-cheha-bhadrācalam. A Brāhmaṇ passing through the wilds of Gooty where the Coya tribes lived, saw a person cooking a snake for food. To his astonishment he was told that the snakes were mere worms; that if he wanted to see a serpant, he would be shown one; and that they (the Coyas) themselves feared no serpants because of the charms which they had received from Ambikes'varar, a *ṛsi* who had told them how to get rid of a large snake. As the Brāhmaṇ desired to see it, he was conducted to the depths of the wilds by a child which carried a winnowing fan and a bundle of straw. On reaching a hole the child set fire to the straw and commenced winnowing the smoke. From out of the bright flames there emerged a monstrous serpant with seven heads. The Brāhmaṇa was struck dumb with fear. He was conducted back, however, by the child and dismissed with gifts in the shape of fruits.[16]

The traditions of S'riṅgavaram near Vizagapatam ascribe the colonization of the wilderness round that locality to one Triśūlabhūpati. Afterwards three classes of wild tribes named S'avarulu (Śabaras), Bhagadulū (Beḍars ?) and Gotamulu chose for themselves a chief called Nīlakaṇṭha, who ruled over all the tribes.[17]

Five septs of wild tribes are said to inhabit the forests of the Jeypore Agency. These are the Miaka-rājas, the Gailutus, the Sagidivandalu, the Sondivan-dalu, and the Ayaraculu.[18]

The Yānādu tribe we have mentioned above, are said to be related to another tribe who have become famous in Buddhist literature. These are the Mallas. The Malla tribe derive their name from living on hills. The Khonds (Gonds ?) call themselves Mallaru (hill people).[19] There were two divisions among the Mallas –the northern Mallas and the southern Mallas. The northern Mallas were evidently the Monedes of Pliny, who with the Suari (S'abaras) occupied the inland country to the south of Palibothra (Pāṭaliputra). Cunningham opined that this was exactly the position of the country of the Muṇḍas and the Suars; and that they must have been the same as the Monedes and the Suari of Pliny. In another passage Pliny mentions the Mandei and the Malli as occupying the country between the Calingae and the Ganges.

In the region inhabited by the Malli there was a mountain named Mallus which Cunningham identified with the mount Maleus of the Mondes and the Suari–the celebrated Mandār hill, to the south of Bhāgalpur, which is fabled to have been used by the gods and demons at the churning of the ocean. The Mandei were thought by Cunningham to be the same as the inhabitants of the Mahānadī which is the Manada of Ptolemy. The Malli or Malei, therefore, were no other than the same people as Ptolemy's Mandalae, who occupied the right bank of the Ganges to the south of Palibothra. It may as well be that they were the people of the Rājmahal Hills who are still called Maler.[20]

The *Mahābhārata* informs us that Bhīma vanquished the southern Mallas and the people of the Bhagavanta mountain.[21] The same epic locates them in the north near the northern Kos'alas.[22] In another connection they are placed after the Yakṛillomanas and before the Sudellas.[23] According to the *Mahāvamso* the chief town of the Mallas was Kus'īnara in modern Nepal.[24]

In the well known drama *Mālavikāgnimitra* we have a sketch of the Beḍars. Parivrājakā relates that at the end of a day's journey, the merchants being exhausted with the toil of the march encamped in a forest. On the king asking her what had happened next, she continues thus :—Then there appeared, striking terror by its first onset, a host of yelling brigands (the Beḍars) whose breasts were crossed by the quiver strap, wearing as a plume peacock's tails that hung down to their ears, bow in hand.[25]

The Kannaḍa poet Bhīma thus describes the Beḍars in the fourteenth century :—

Like darkness personified, like moving blue mountains, like hills of lamp-black that had (the advantage of) hands and feet, like walls of iron, like herds of elephants that could speak, and like black (Kṛṣṇa) serpents that had their hoods shrunk, the Beḍars came in groups to that place :—

> Oḍalugoṇḍa tamandha-paṭalavo naḍeva-nilādrigaḷo kai-kā ।
> l–paḍeda kajjala-girigaḷo karbbonna-bhittigaḷo ॥
> nuḍigalita mātaṅga saṅghavo heḍey-uḍugida sita-ahigaḷo ena– ।
> l–eḍe–viḍade saṅdaṇisi Beḍaru bandar-ā-eḍege. ॥ [26]

Another Kannaḍa poet who has described the Beḍara women is Virūpakṣa (circa A. D. 1519) :—

The group of Beḍara (*vyādha*) women moved on with their teeth sparkling like the flashes of a side glance, and surpassing the redness of their feet, and there bodies darker than their locks of hair :—

> Kaḍegaṇṇa kāntige-orageyāda pal-kadir-aḍi keṁpa murid-adhara kāṅti ।
> muḍi-kappa kiḷ-māḍuva pogariṅda naḍeduḍu Biyaḍa peṇgaḷa taṇḍa ॥ [27]

No section of the wild tribes gave such infinite trouble to the Hindu kingdoms as the Beḍars. Somewhere in the early seventh century A. D., we hear of the growing menace that was to be the cause of commotion in the Karṇāṭaka kingdoms for centuries to come. It was just this time when, as related above, the Kirātas and tribes akin to them had moved down to the Vindhyan region along the spurs of the Aravali Hills. An inscription dated only in the Cālukya-Vikrama era relates the death of Aṇḍige Mādaya in a fight with the Beḍars, while they were ascending a hill.[28] The Gaddemane stone inscription, ascribed to about the seventh century A. D., relates that when Śilāditya ascended the throne, Pettaṇi Satyaṅka pierced through the thick of the battle with the brave Beḍara Rāya and died. This stone record was found in the Sagara hobli.[29] From this we may surmise that the Beḍars had already succeeded in securing a firm footing in the mountainous parts of the Karṇāṭaka by the seventh century A. D.

Their depradations increased during the times of the Rāṣṭrakūṭas. In the reign of the Rāṣṭrakūṭa king Kannara Deva, as is related in a record dated A. D. 954, Banavāse Twelve Thousand was under Rasaṇṇa, son of Kalivittarasa, while Kaṅga Liṇḍiga held the nāḷ-gāvuṇḍ-ship of the same district. Just then the Beḍar robbers carried off the sacred cows; and the *gāvuṇḍa* (perhaps the *ūr-gāvuṇḍa*, who is not mentioned in the inscription) attacked them. But this brave man, who had the *birudu* of *Ornament of the Kacchavikula,* died in the fight.[30]

The name of the locality to which the sacred cows belonged is not given in the epigraph. But from the following we gather that it was Kūḍali, an *agra-*

hāra village and a centre of Brāhmaṇa activity. The *vīragal* (hero memorial stone) which gives us these details, is dated A. D. 955. The ruler was the same Rāṣṭrakūṭa king Kannara Deva III. But over Banavāse-nāḍu there was placed Javanaiśa, and the nāḷ-gāvuṇḍship was entrusted to Biṭṭiga, while the ūr-gāvuṇḍship was under Seśigaḷa Būva. The Beḍars, who had attacked Kūḍali in the previous year, and evidently got off free, now raided the same Kūḍali *agrahāra* village and carried off the cows. Seśigaḷa Būva recovered the cows at the Maseyara boundary but died in the struggle. His son commemorated this brave deed of his father in the above *vīragal*.[31]

For ten years the Beḍars left Kūḍali to itself. But in A. D. 965, as is related in the inscription dated in that year of the reign of the same Rāṣṭrakūṭa monarch, when Javanaiśa and Biṭṭiga continued respectively in their *nāḍ* and *ūr gāvuṇḍa* offices, the Beḍars raided again Kūḍali and lifted the cows. But some one - obviously the *ūr-gāvuṇḍa* whose name is defaced in the record-, "fought like Arjuna", recovered the cows but died in the fight in such a manner as to receive a *vīragal* at the hands of his son.[32]

In A. D. 977 the Beḍars attacked a town (in the Nāgamaṅgala tāluka ?), the name of which is incompletely given in the inscription, and carried off the women. A brave citizen named Gavare S'eṭṭi, "fearing not the Beḍar forces," fell upon them but died in the struggle.[33]

The government of the Western Cālukyas was faced with the same danger which had confronted the Rāṣṭrakūṭas. From mere cattle-lifters the Beḍars had gradually assumed the proportions of hill-chieftains (*maleparu*), and even dared to ally themselves with the avowed enemies of the Western Cālukyas. They continued to harass the Western Cālukya territories from about A. D. 1033 till A. D. 1092. The Western Cālukya monarch Jayasiṁha III, also known as Jagadekamalla I, had ascended the throne in about A. D. 1018-9. His rule lasted till about A. D. 1042.[34]

There were three raids within this brief period. In about A. D. 1033 occurred a series of insurrections and raids in the Western Cālukya state. Ālayya had been placed in that year over the Banavāse Twelve Thousand. But the credit of putting down the enemies belongs to his gallant son Jayasiṅgha Deva. The inscription which gives us these and other details, describes graphically his brave deeds thus:— When he took the field the Malcvar (*i. e.*, the Hill Chieftains) shrivelled up, the Manneyar trembled, the Sāmantas' hearts failed, the Maṇḍalikas were alarmed, the Beḍars cried, and the Kurumbars were scared. By the might of his single arm he raised up the earth, and laying four fingers lightly on the back of his people, he gained the world by his valour-Simhabhūpati ! No wonder this hero received the title of *Munn-iṟivan* (Slayer in front of the van) because of his valour.[35]

King Jayasiṁha III had two brothers in his service whose gallant deeds have come down to history. One of them was the *Mahāmaṇḍaleśvara* Bijjalabhūpa (Bijjarasa). Two inscriptions describe his bravery thus in A. D. 1042:— This warrior in half a moment captured Toragale, attacked and seized Bhaṭṭa, without fear plucked up the Beyḍars (*i. e.*, the Beḍars) by the root, and gained the name that he alone was Torahara Māri (*neṟad iral aṭṭi muṭṭi piḍid ōrade Byeḍara bēran eyide kiḷt.*)[36]

His younger brother Goṇarasa emulated him in the matter of freeing the State from the Beḍars. In the same year (A. D. 1042) Goṇarasa drove out the Maleyavar of the Seven Male.[37]

Local officers with the closest co-operation of the authorities dealt with the Beḍars during the times of the Western Cālukyas. This explains why the names of all the officials including that of the monarch himself, are given along with that of the hero–himself a local officer– in the following epigraph describing the action taken against the wild tribes. It was in the year A. D. 1058 when the king was the Western Cālukya Someśvara I, also called Trailokyamalla and Āhavamalla (A. D. 1042–1068), that there occurred a daring Beḍar raid. The Cālukya Gaṅga Permmāṇadi Vikramāditya, the future glorious Vikramāditya VI,[38] was the viceroy over the Gaṅgavāḍi Ninety-Six Thousand, ruling from his capital Baḷḷigāve; the Perggaḍe Nārāyaṇa-ayya, the chief of the Karaṇams, was enjoying (*anubhavisuttam ire*) the Banavase Twelve Thousand; Arasimayya of the Jiḍḍuḷige Seventy was the *nāḷ-gāvuṇḍa*; and the ūr-gāvuṇḍship had been entrusted to Mācaya, son of Goggi S'eṭṭi of Aḍigaṭṭe.

As the record dated above narrates, "Hearing the outcry that a force of Beḍars had penetrated into Muḍyangeri, seized the cows, and dishonoured (lit. unloosened the waists of) women, - not disregarding it, Māci Gāvuṇḍa attacked and fell upon them, and thinking that the meaning of the verse 'The victor gains spoils, the slain too, the celestial nymph: what fear, then, of death in war to him who for a moment seeks the close encounter?'–applied it to his own fate, he carried on the fight to the end, taunted the manliness of the opposing force, recovered the cows in Belagavatti, and killing many, gained the world of gods as a mighty champion". The relatives he left behind received the usual honours of war relief in the shape of a *nettaru-goḍige.*[39]

Three years later in S'aka 983 (A. D. 1061-2) the Beḍars again raided one of the Western Cālukya towns. Jakkayya of the family of Barmma-deva,[40] in his attempt to rescue the cattle carried off by the Beḍars, lost his life.[41]

Even in the reign of the celebrated Vikramāditya VI, also known as Vikramāṅka Tribhuvanamalla II, who reigned from A. D. 1073 till A. D. 1126-7,[42] the Beḍars raised their heads again. Sometimes they raided as mere cattle-lifters, and once they joined hands with the enemies of the Western Cālukyas, the Raṭṭas. It was in A. D. 1092-3 that the hill chiefs laid siege to Kiriyamāguṇḍa, which was in the service of the god Tripurāntaka, captured the cows (*Kiriya-māguṇḍiya Maleparu mutti turuvan koṇḍu*), unloosened the waists of women and departed. Tailama, son of Kāci S'eṭṭi, was able to recover the cows although he died of the effects of dagger thrusts.[43]

The Beḍars were invited by the Raṭṭas to plunder the dominions of the Western Cālukyas. In A. D. 1102 the armies of five Beḍar kings led by Vibharasa advanced on the Western Cālukya territory, and besieged Hāruvanahaḷḷi and Kedāra. The king's soldiers, so we are told in the record dated above, without taking food chastised a thousand braves and took their lives. If the rank and file of the Western Cālukya army showed such exemplary bravery, their leaders also could boast of a similar record. Kaleya Nāyaka, who we may surmise was probably the *ūr-gāvaṇḍa* of the locality, had been given the lead. But he turned back fatigued. His son-in-law Bijjala Nāyaka at once followed him, " and pleasing him, begged for the post of danger, and fighting with the five Beḍar kings," beat them, although he died gloriously in the battle.[44]

The next year (A. D. 1103) witnessed another Beḍar incursion. This time Kedāra was besieged by the Beḍar army under Vaḍera Ēcarasa. The Beḍar chieftain had ventured to attack even the camp (*bīḍu*) (of the viceroy the Mahāmaṇḍaleśvara Permmāṇadi Deva ?). Just then Bībaya Nāyaka, son-in-law of Mallayya Kariyaka Nāyaka, came to the rescue of the town. He was a champion beloved by the army, as the record narrates. Leaving Hāruvanahaḷḷi (behind ?), he surrounded the Beḍar army at Kedāra, and fighting with the Beḍar Aybarasa, evidently the general of the Beḍar king Vaḍera Ēcarasa, slew him but lost his own life in the battle.[45]

In the above instances we have a significant fact–the Beḍar chieftains who, in the earlier years had been only cattle-lifters, had now one or two leaders who had risen to the position of kings, as the names Vibharasa, Vaḍera (*i. e.*, probably Oḍeyar) Ēcarasa, and Aybarasa clearly denote.

None but the Beḍars could have been responsible for the cattle raid in the Brāhman village of Nelavatti in A. D. 1125. The inscription which gives us the following details, does not, it must be confessed, expressly mention the Beḍars; but from the facts we have cited above, it can easily be inferred that Dese of Helagavatti, who attacked the cows of Nelavatti, could only have been a Beḍar chieftain. The *agrahāra* of Nelavatti, however, was not without its heroes. The tailor Padma's son Cikka recovered the cows but died fighting against the cattle robbers.[46]

The Jiḍḍulige Seventy province was the next objective of the Beḍars. The *Mahāmaṇḍaleśvara*

Ekkalarasa Deva was ruling in that province in A. D. 1130. Sindhi Devarasa, evidently a Beḍar king, entered āyile in the Jiḍḍulige Seventy and carried off the cows. But Billoja attacked the invaders, recovered the cows, and died in the struggle.[47] Māyile suffered further hardships in about A. D. 1115 when Kāḷarasa, another Beḍar chieftain. carried off the cows. But once again the hero who recovered the cows, Utta Gāvuṇḍa, died fighting.[48]

That the Western Cālukyas did not succeed in uprooting the Beḍar evil is clear from the events that took place not only in A. D. 1156 under the Western Cālukya ruler Tailapa, also called Trailokyamalla, who ruled from A. D. 1150 till A. D. 1182, but also from the trend of events under the Kaḷacuriyas. In A. D. 1156 Madasāle Kāḷarasa raided Korakoḍa, a village of the immemorial *agrahāra* Kuppagaḍe. But Deva Gāvuṇḍa and Malla Gāvuṇḍa shone by their courage in recovering the cows.[49]

One fact stands out prominently in the history of the Beḍar raids given above: although occasionally we hear of the royal troops coming to the rescue of the citizens, yet the duty of defending the honour of women and of recovering the cows was primarily the work of the Gāvuṇḍas of the locality. The noble tradition of entrusting the work of protecting the home and the hearth of the people into the hands of the Vais ya and the S'ūdra classes was transmitted to the later ages as one of the most abiding treasures of early Karṇāṭaka culture and history.

When we come to the Kaḷacuriya times, we find the same high sense of honour and gallantry in the minds of the non-warrior classes. In A. D. 1160 Kallarasa laid siege to the well known *agrahāra* of Jambūr. It was in the reign of the Kaḷacuriya king Bijjala Deva (A. D. 1156- A. D. 1167). The hero who killed many of the enemy, although he died in the attempt, was the fisherman Biṭṭeya.[50] The failure of the Kaḷacuriya Government to deal satisfactorily with this Beḍar maraudar Kāḷarasa is seen in A. D. 1165 when he united with Das'aratha Daṇḍanātha, and " according to the custom of the class ", " by means of plundering ", carried of the cows of Hosavaḷḷi. Das'aratha Daṇḍanātha, inspite of his high-sounding title, was evidently a Beḍar. Against the two marched "the good warrior Kāḷiga" who, performing various deeds of valour (described in the epigraph), died in the fight.[51] Kāḷiga could only have been a Gāvuṇḍa.

But Karṇāṭaka history also contains instances of a few Gāvuṇḍas who committed cattle raids. Among such was Singada Manca Gauḍa of Biṭṭeyūr, who penetrated into the town of Jambūr, dishonoured the women, and carried off the cows, as is narrated in a record of A. D. 1175 of the times of the Kaḷacuriya king Rāya Murāri Soyi Deva. Whether Singada Manca Gauḍa was himself a Beḍar or had sought the aid of the Beḍars in perpetrating this cowardly deed, we cannot make out. But the fisherman Bāceya fought against him, killed many although he lost his life thereby.[52]

The other raid in A. D. 1177 in the reign of the same monarch, was undoubtedly the work of a Beḍar chieftain, although like Singada Manca Gauḍa, he went under an apparently honoured title. In that year Vikramāṅka was the governor over Banavāse-nāḍ. The wretched Gāvuṇḍasvāmi, a Beḍar, no doubt, attacked the famous Kuppaṭṭūr *agrahāra*, made prisoners many Brāhmaṇs, besieged the village in three circles, plundered it and unloosened the waists of women. But the brave Ketaya Nāyaka recovered the women and the live stock, fought like Māri but died in the encounter.[53]

Although they continued to be cattle-lifters for a long time to come, as we shall narrate presently, yet the Beḍars showed signs of a change that was gradually coming over them. This was in the form of a firm hold which they acquired not only in the hilly regions of the Karṇāṭaka but also of the Tamil land as well. The history of their activities in the Tamil country brings us to the elucidation of another name by which they were known-that of Bhills or Villavars. According to Hindu authors, no distinction was made between a Bhilla, a S'ābara, and a Kirāta. Thus in the *Das'akumāracarita* we find them mentioned as identical tribes.[54] This confusion between a Bhilla and a S'abara is not altogether unintelligible. The Koragars of South Kanara are Bhills although, as we have seen above, one particular tribe among them called Soppu Koragars belongs to the S'abara group. These Bhills are not confined to the southern and western parts of the country. They are met with also in Bengal.[55]

But we are concerned with their activities on the western and southern coasts.[56] The Villavars of Tamil history were essentially bowmen and not, as Rice remarked, Ceras; and as such belonged to the large group of wild tribes who form the subject of this treatise.[57] The greatness of Rājarāja Deva Jayaṅgoṇḍa Coḷa is sung in A. D. 1046 thus:— That before him the guilty Villavar ailing with bowel complaint, fled from his dominions and hid himself in the jungles.[58] In A. D. 1080 it is said that Kulottuṅga Coḷa Deva " caused the wheel of his authority to roll over all regions, so that the Villavars lost their position[59] The same phrase is repeated in an inscription dated A. D. 1089 of the same monarch.[60] In the records ranging from A. D. 1095 till A. D. 1099 Kulottuṅga Coḷa Deva is said to have destroyed the Villavars.[61] The fact of the subjugation of the Villavars by that monarch is further borne out in epigraphs dated A. D. 1110 and 1118 which sing his praise and say that when he caused the wheel of his authority to roll over all regions, the Villavars became disconcerted.[62]

That Rice's contention that the Villavars were Ceras is unintelligible, inspite of their having a bow on their standard, is seen when we find tribes belonging to the Villavar stock inhabiting other parts of the country under the name of Billavars or Bhills or Bheels. The Billavars inhabit South Kanara and are now a part of the progressive section of the people Their ancient vocation was that of tapping toddy from the cocoanut and palm trees. They are the same as the Kumāra Paikas (Junior Foot) of Honnāvūru and the Haḷe Paikas (Old Foot) of the Karṇāṭaka regions.[63] But the traditions of either South or North Kanara have nothing of importance to say concerning their interference in contemporary politics.

We, therefore, have to go to the history of Gujarat and Rajputana to glean something about their contribution to the annals of the land. One of the most notorious names in early Gujarat history is that Graha Ripoo (Gṛha Ripu ?), who lived at Vāmanasthali under the shadow of Mount Gīrnār but near the coast. He despised Brahmans and plundered the people passing along the road. He was called the *Barbarian, One who hunted upon Gīrnār, ate the flesh of cows, drank spirituous liquor*, and *passed and repassed the ocean.*[64] These qualifications are enough to stamp him as a Mleccha chieftain. That he was a Bhill is suggested by the names of his allies and tributary chieftains among whom were a great many " Bheels "[65]

Another famous name in Gujarat history is that of Vana Rāja. This Cāwura chieftain, as his name signifies, was perhaps of Bhilla stock. A little digression into his antecedents will make the point clear. It is said that Sāmant Singh, one of the slaves of Raja Phūr (Porus)- Deva Rāja of Kanouj-having committed some fault, was put to death by the king. At the same time his house was plundered, and his wife, then pregnant, fled towards Gujarat. Here in the new country she bore a son who was discovered in the wilderness of Gujarat by Rāja S'īl Deva, a local ruler, who took the child to Pālanpūr and reared him up. This child arriving at man's age, took to evil company, and finally turned out into a highwayman. Some time later, he seized the royal treasure going from Gujarat to Kanouj and took shelter in the mountain fastnesses in order to escape the vengeance of the king of Kanouj. But, so the story runs, a marketman named Cam̐pa weaned him from his evil propensities. He then assumed the name of Banraj or Bansraj (Vana Rāja), founded the famous city of Paṭaṇ which continued to be the royal residence of the Gujarat rulers till the transference of the government to Ahmedābād.[66]

Since we cannot conceive of a local ruler suddenly finding a child in the wilderness, and since it is impossible that a child should have continually taken to evil ways if it had not the Bhilla or Kirāta blood in its veins, we have to dispense with the above account which makes Vana Rāja the son of a Rajput slave as the attempt of chroniclers to give a classical colouring to persons that had really no title to honour except that of inherent valour. We have seen elsewhere how rulers with no claims whatsoever for Kṣatriyahood have been classed among Kṣatriyas. Vana Rāja belongs to this group of rulers.

The unreliability of the story of his Rajput parentage is apparent not only from what we have said above but also from the following considerations: when Vana Raja had resolved upon founding the city of Paṭaṇ, he went in search of a site suited for the amusement of the chase. He met a shepherd who told him where a suitable site could be found. The shepherd whose name was Anhil, stipulated that the city should be named after him, saying at the same time that he had there seen a hare beat a dog by her exertion and agility. Here was laid the foundation of Anhilwārāh (Anhilwāḍ) which was rechristened Nahrwālah, and which finally came to be known as Paṭaṇ (Skt. Paṭṭaṇa). The date of the foundation of Paṭaṇ, we may note by the way, is assigned by some to A. D. 747, and by others to A. D. 817.[67]

Now, the story of the hare and the dog is a legend that is common to many kingdoms in the Deccan and the south, and upon which no reliance whatsoever can be placed. To give only two examples, we are told in the *Tazkirāt-ul-Mulūk* that the Bāhmani Sultan Ahmad Shāh (A. D. 1422- A. D. 1435) made Bidar his capital because he was likewise guided by the behaviour of a hare.[68] The origin of the celebrated city of Vijayanagara is also traced to a similar incident; and, as we said in connection with the history of that city, the legend of the hare and the dog is worthless for any historical purpose.[69] We see, therefore, how untrustworthy is the account which masquerades the Bhilla Vana Rāja under the garb of a Rajput.

The *Rās Māla* which gives us the above account of Vana Rāja, also contains some interesting facts concerning the Bhills. It is said of the well known Siddh Rāja that, once while returning from Mālwā, he was obstructed by a force of the Bhills "against whom none could fight." It was only the timely arrival of his minister Sāmtoo with an army from Gujarat that saved the king from a precarious predicament.[70]

The Bhills occupied Mewār too. And the history of Rajputana relates that Bappa, as an early Gohila chief was familiarly called, established his power after overthrowing the Bhills.[71]

The Bhills spread themselves over Khāṇḍeṣ as well.[72]

We return to the history of the south and the west. In A. D. 1004 occurred an event of the first magnitude in the annals of the Karṇāṭaka kingdoms. In that year Rājendra Coḷa, son of the great Rājarāja and commander of the Coḷa army, captured Talakāḍ, the Gaṅga capital, and brought the ancient Gaṅga power to an end.[73] In a series of masterly strokes, the Coḷas contemplated the conquest of the entire Karṇāṭaka; and as first steps to their magnificent scheme, fixed the outposts of the Coḷa influence from Arkalgūḍ in the west, through Seringapatam, north by Nelamaṅgalam as far as Niḍugal, to Heñjūru in the extreme south,[74] in such a manner as to threaten the extinction of Karnāṭaka as an ancient historical and cultural unit.

It was at this juncture that the wild tribes- now under the more dignified designation of Malepas, unconsciously came to the rescue of the country. We have seen how from the seventh century onwards, the

Beḍars continued to harass the citizens of the *agrahāras*; and how one or two names among their chiefs suggested the assumption of some sort of regal power by them. One of the earliest references to their principality is to be found in a record dated A. D. 887 which speaks of the Male Thousand (and its people) being the guardians of a grant of the Gaṅga king Satyavākya Koṅguṇivarma.[75]

Ninety years later (in A. D. 977) we come across four chiefs of the Malepas in a record of that date of the times of king Rakkasa Gaṅga. They are styled the *nālvar Malepar* and are included among the guardians of the royal grant.[76] That the Malepa chiefs, and simultaneously with them a family which also belonged essentially to the Malepa stock, offered the Coḷā general stout resistance is proved by the following inscription relating to him. It is dated A. D. 1006-7 and it narrates that Aprameya, the lord of Kottamaṇḍala, and the general of Rājarāja Deva, was the "Destruction to the race of the hill chiefs (*Malepa-kuḷa-kāḷam*.)"

But in the same year that general encountered the Hoysala army under Nāgaṇḍā, the minister of Poysala (Hoysala), the founder of the Hoysala line, and won a victory over it and other Hoysala generals at Kalavūr (mod. Kaleyūr near Mālingi, opposite to Talakāḍ on the other side of the river.)[77] But the Coḷa career of conquest in the Karnāṭaka was not destined to live long.

That General Aprameya's claim to have destroyed the race of hill chiefs was by no means entirely admissible is proved by the following epigraphs which describe the activities of the Malepas ranging over a century. A record dated A. D. 1068 praises thus the greatness of General Lakṣmaṇa under the western Cālukya king Bhuvanaikamalla Someśvara :- "Assaulting the Koṅkaṇa, he is treading it down like his stirrup; driving back the Seven Kombu, he pursues and catches them; the Seven Male he makes it to bend down, breaks and uproots them; thus saying, the hill chiefs, without showing (or lifting) their heads, agree to what king Rāyagaṇḍa Gopāla says before he speaks-how great is he !"[78] General Lakṣmaṇa, or as he was also called Rāyagaṇḍa Gopāla, Governor over Banavāse, had, therefore, broken the power of the hill chiefs of Seven Male- a region which we are unable to identify before earning the above praise.

The middle classes in the Karṇāṭaka in the eleventh century maintained the traditions prevalent in the tenth century of opposing cattle-lifters who swept over the plains from the hills. We may recall here the heroic deeds of Tailama, son of Kāci S'eṭṭi, in A. D. 1092 mentioned above.

The title assumed by General Govinda, under the Pāṇḍya ruler Tribhuvanamalla Kāma Deva, as recorded in an inscription of A.D. 1113, *viz.*, that of gambler of the Malepas (*Malepara jūju*),[79] proves that the hill chiefs were still active in the first quarter of the twelth century.

Our surmise is further substantiated by a record dated A. D. 1129 of the reign of the Western Cālukya king Somes'vara III (A. D. 1126–A. D. 1138) which sings the praise of the monarch thus :—" As soon as he began to walk, the hostile chiefs began to walk away into the forest through fear; as soon as he began to talk, their talk was confined to the wild men of the jungle (*naḍe-galal oḍarisal ātaṃ naḍe-galal oḍarisidar ahitar aḍavige bhayadiṃ nuḍigalal oḍarisi begam nuḍigalal oḍarisidar ari nripar vana-cararōḷ*).[80] More substantial proof of the existence of the Malepas in the twelfth century is afforded by the epigraphs of the Hoysala kings which we shall presently enumerate.

The Hoysalas blocked the Tamilian advance in the Karṇāṭaka. These new rulers were themselves of the Malepa stock. Fleet's assertion that they "belonged to the lineage of Yadu,"[81] is hardly convincing. On the other hand, the statement of Rice that they were of indigenous origin is correct. Their birth place was Sosevūru, Sanskritized into S'as'ākapura. Rice identified it with Aṅgaḍi on the Western Ghats, in the Mūḍigere tāluka.[82] The title which they bore–that of *Maleparoḷ Gaṇḍan* (Champion over Hill Chiefs)—appears not only among their *birudus* in their numerous inscriptions but was also their sign-manual, and it is also seen in their coins. This itself proves, as Rice remarked, that they were a family of hill chiefs to start with on the Western Ghats; and that the conquest of the most prominent hill chiefs–whom unfortunately we cannot identify for the present–was a noticeable feature in their progress as sovereigns over the Karṇāṭaka.[83]

The honour of turning back the Tamil arms falls to the lot of the Hoysala ruler Nṛpa Kāma. In A. D. 1022, and again in A. D. 1026, he opposed the Kongālvas who were the allies of the Coḷa rulers, and with this defeat, the Tamilian retreat from the Karṇāṭaka may be said to begin. The final expulsion of the Coḷas from the Karṇāṭaka soil was effected, however, only in A. D. 1116, when the Hoysala general Gaṅga Rāja recovered Talakāḍ from the Tamilians.[84]

We may now rapidly survey the vast range of Hoysala records in order to establish the validity of the claims of the Hoysalas to be called *Maleparoḷ*

Gaṇḍan. Of the time of Sāla, the progenitor of the line, and from whom the Hoysalas received their name,[85] we have no record. It is only in A. D. 1006 that the word Poysala occurs as the name of the king whose minister was Nāgaṇṇa.[86] There is no evidence to prove that Hoysala assumed the *birudu of Maleparoḷ Gaṇḍan.* Neither is there any proof to show that that *birudu* was included among the titles of Nṛpa Kāma also called Kāma Hoysala.[87] Thus we may assert that till the days of Nṛpa Kāma, the Hoysalas did not succeed in becoming *Champions over the Malepas.*

In A. D. 1090, however, we are told that a Poysala Deva called himself *Maleparoḷ Gaṇḍan.*[88] This is repeated in a record of A. D. 1095.[89] And in A. D. 1110 or thereabouts a ruler called Vīra Gaṅga Hoysala Deva is called by the same *birudu.*[90] These three inscriptions refer to Vinayāditya Hoysala Deva Tribhuvanamalla, the first notable figure in Hoysala history. Although he was a feudatory of the famous Western Cālukya king Vikramāditya VI, yet he had a powerful kingdom which included within its boundaries hilly regions like the Bayalnāḍ and the like.[91] Since A. D. 1090 is the earliest date which refers to the championship of the Hoysala ruler over the Malepas, it may be assumed that it was about this year that the issue between the other Malepas-who may have been the descendants of the Four Malepas we have noted above-, and the worshippers of the goddess Vāsantikā-as the Hoysalas called themselves-, was finally decided resulting in a signal victory for the latter justifying their *birudu* of *Maleparoḷ Gaṇḍan.*

A few more instances of rulers who continued to prefix this *birudu* after king Vinayāditya's time may suffice to prove how it came to stay in Hoysala history. Among the *birudus* of the famous Viṣṇuvardhana Deva, as recorded in an inscription dated A. D. 1117, were the following :- *Maleparoḷ Gaṇḍādi aneka nāmāvaḷi samālaṅkritar appa* (one who was adorned with the title of *Maleparoḷ Gaṇḍa* and other numerous titles).[92] Viṣṇuvardhana Deva is said to have been " a royal kite to destroy the serpent Cengiri, Rāya of the Male-rājas, " in an inscription of A. D. 1160.[93]

Vīra Narasiṁha Hoysala Deva, in a record dated about A. D. 1160, is called King of the Hill Kings (*malerāja-rājan*) in addition to the *birudu* of *Maleparoḷ Gaṇḍan*.[94] The latter title along with the *birudu* of a *Male Bheruṇḍa* is given in A. D. 1196 to Ballāḷa Deva II.[95] In A. D. 1218 the same monarch is called by the accredited *birudu* as well as by that of *Rājā of the Male Rājas*.[96] Narasiṁha Deva II is called *Maleparoḷ Gaṇḍan* in a record of A. D. 1135, and again in an inscription of A. D. 1276.[97] Vīra Narasiṁha III is styled in A. D. 1276, and again in about A. D. 1285, *A King over the Hill Kings*, *Maleparoḷ Gaṇḍan*, and *Male Bheruṇḍa.* These titles were given also to Vīra Ballāḷa III in A. D. 1321.[98]

Notwithstanding the fact of the Hoysalas having been *Champions over Hill Chiefs*, they were unable, to use the expression we have met with in an inscription, to pluck the Beḍers by the roots. Hence we find in their times Beḍar attacks as before. Vinayāditya Hoysala, who in our opinion was the first to assume the *birudu* of *Maleparoḷ Gaṇḍan*, himself had to confront the opposition of the Malepas. We infer this from the following inscription dated A. D. 1123 which describes his diplomatic attitude towards them thus :- " On the heads of the Malepas who growing proud, oppose him, he lays his sword; on the heads of the Malepas who filled with fear do not grow proud or oppose him, he at once lays his hand-Vinayāditya."[99]

That this double method of dealing with the Malepas *viz.*, of showing them consideration where it ought to be shown, and of punishing them when they grew turbulent—was indeed the policy of Vinayāditya Poysala is proved by two later records. One is dated A. D. 1184 which repeats the above in the statement that he brought his sword down on the hill chiefs who were proud and opposed him, and put his hand on the heads of hill chiefs who were not proud and who submitted to him :—

Balidaḍe maledaḍe Malepara taleyoḷu bāḷ iḍuvan udita-bhaya-rasavasadim

baliyada maleyada Malepara taleyoḷu kaiy iḍuvan oḍane Vinayādityam.[100]

Another inscription of the reign of Narasiṃha Deva dated A. D. 1205 narrates that "all the sons of the hill kings, rubbing their heads, rose up, and cast themselves at his lotus feet. On the heads of those who would not submit, he laid his sword; on the heads of those who yielded, he laid his hand." [101] Further, an inscription dated A. D. 1138 relates that in the breasts and brains of the Malepas, did the fear of Vinayāditya spread, when he lifted his hands to smite the heads of the Malepas.[102]

A *vīragal* dated A. D. 1136 found in Maraḷe, Chikmagalur tāluka, of the times of his illustrious grandson, Viṣṇuvardhana Deva, confirms our surmise that the Hoysala Government was still confronted with the Malepa evil. This *vīragal* commemorates the death of the gallant Bamma when he killed many of the Malepas who had raided the village of Maraḷe and dishonoured women.[103]

The reign of Ballāḷa Deva II (A. D. 1173-1220) witnessed the inability of the State to cope with the increasing Beḍar danger. There were four Beḍar raids in the reign of this monarch. In about A. D. 1186 when the great minister Pratipanna Sārasūryya Deva Daṇṇāyaka was ruling over Taladi, the *nāḷ-gāvuṇḍa* being Kanasoge Yaṛa Kavi Gavuḍa, Pancāla Būta killed the herdsmen and carried off the cows (of Kanasoge ?). But the *nāḷ-gāvuṇḍa*'s younger brother Ēca Gavuḍa fought with the raiders and recovered the cows, although he died in the fight.[104] Another instance of a Gāvuṇḍa fighting against the Beḍars is that of Madi Gauḍa, son of Billahaḷḷi Billa Gauḍa, in A. D. 1200. He too suffered the death of a hero.[105]

An equally courageous instance of a citizen in the same reign is that of Vaijarasa. In A. D. 1202 when Aggada-rāya, evidently a Beḍar chief, ran off into the Beḍarabanki forest, in front of Hemmāḍi, Vaijarasa pierced his skull with a single arrow and won the title of *Kaṇṇambu* (Eye-arrow) from the king.[106]

The most conspicuous example of bravery in the reign of the same monarch is that of Cila Gauḍa, son of Hariya Rāmaya Gauḍa of Āsaṅdi-nāḍ. In A. D. 1209 the Beḍars penetrated into Beḷa Gāvuṇḍa's village Kallakere and departed (causing the usual havoc). Cila Gauḍa ran to the fight, attacked the Beḍar elephant, recovered the cows and with great valour captured the Kirāta army in Kharggakeṭaka. For having caused that village to rejoice, he "received the worship of the people as having the fortune of a hero."[107]

One of the main reasons why the Hoysala Government did not succeed in eliminating the Beḍar and the Malepar element from their kingdom was due perhaps to the fact that it was spread far and wide over other regions as well. The Yādavas of Devagiri, for instance, likewise had to slove the Beḍar problem. In A. D. 1216 Māyi Deva Daṇṇāyaka was the Superintendent over the Banavāse-nāḍ under the Yādava Nārāyaṇa Siṁhaḷa Deva. And Iśvara Devarasa, son of Malla Nṛpāla of the Phaṇivaṁśa, was in Belagavatti. In this town (?) there occurred a great fight with the Beḍars which is thus graphically described in the epigraph:— The Mādanabāga Beḍars raided (Belagavatti) and carried off the cows. Then Iśvara Devarasa ordered Ciṇṇaya Sāhani to meet them. "Like an angry Yama, the Paṭṭa Sāhani Ciṇṇa pursued them. Hastening after them, on coming in sight of the Beḍar force, he shouted, and charging on his horse which was as fleet as the wind, he played at ball with their heads, and performed astonishing feats, recovered the cows and made a feast for the kites." It is no wonder that the scribe, who thus describes the heroism of Ciṇṇaya Sāhani in A. D. 1216, asks the question at the end of the epigraph– "Who had a servant like Ciṇṇaya (was) to Iśvara Deva ?" In what manner the State appreciated the bravery of the people who, like Ciṇṇaya Sāhani, fell in the service of the Government is seen in the method in which Iśvara Deva rewarded Ciṇṇaya's descendants. War relief called *diṅgariga-vṛtti* (servants' means of livelihood) was granted by the ruler to Ciṇṇaya's son and younger brother as a perpetual endowment.[108]

The Brāhman settlements called *agrahāras* were often raided. Thus the immemorial *agrahāra* Marasūr, on the boundary of Nelkudure, was attacked by a Beḍar force in A. D. 1242. But Bommayya Nāyaka, son of

Somayya, attacked Duggi S'eṭṭi, who is described as the strong man of the enemy Beḍar's force, and slew him, although he himself died in the struggle.[109]

That the *agrahāras* were in constant danger of the Beḍars is further borne out by a clause in a *samaya-patra* (or document relating to land) which all the Brahmans of the great *agrahāra* Amṛtake-s'avapura *alias* Kūṭanamaḍuvu made in about A. D. 1291, in the presence of the great minister Harihara Daṇṇāyaka. The agreement ran thus:—"Fines, faults, plunder by Beḍars, trouble from robbers, belong to the Brāhmaṇs of the several villages; the three hundred (*i. e.*, those of the *agrahāra* Amṛitakes'avapura) have nothing to do with them."[110] This once again proves the assertion we have here and elsewhere made that the care of the local units was entrusted to the villagers themselves, the central power exercising general supervision over the affairs of the local bodies.

We shall give one more instance of the Beḍar raids before we pass on to their activities in the Empire of Vijayanagara. This refers to about A. D. 1300, and it occurred under the *regime* of the *Mahāsāmanta* Sovaṇṇa Daṇṇāyaka. The defaced inscription which gives us these details, relates that some one came and carried off the *kalas'a* of the temple of Harihara. The Beḍars attacked him in return in Kañciyagere but he slew many of the Beḍars and fell in the fight.[111]

Both the dangers which had confronted the gallant old Hoysala monarch Vīra Ballāḷa Deva III.,—*viz.*, that of the Beḍars and that of the Muhammadans—were transmitted to his celebrated successors-the founders of the Empire of Vijayanagara. Of these we are concerned here only with the former which the earliest rulers themsleves had to meet. Harihara I, was attacked by the Beḍars.[112] But the five brothers were destined to play a great part in the history of the country and the Beḍar attack was evidently crushed.

An inscription wrongly dated A. D. 1228 but which may be assigned to A. D. 1408 of the reign of Deva Rāya.I, gives an account of a spirited struggle by the trusted servants of the State. Vīraṇṇa Oḍeyar was the Viceroy over the Āraga Eighteen Kampaṇa which was also called Male Rājya. A Beḍar chief named Boḷeya Mummeya Nāyaka having slaughtered all over the country, carried off prisoners, and caused great disturbance and famine in the kingdom. The king being anxious for the safety of the subjects, promptly gave an order saying that the Beḍar was to be brought to proper order (*ā Beḍarige takka ājñeyanu māḍuvudu endu*). The Viceroy at once raised a force and coming against that Beḍar leader, gave order in Ānaveri-nāḍ to assemble all the available horse and foot.

At this moment came forward the heroes of the locality led by Aṅgada Rājamalla Mahāprabhu, the Hallināḍu Keyura Nāḍiga (with various titles), the people of Haratāḷu, Modūr, Kallūr, Keḷale, Dānamūla, with Haratāḷu Medi Gauḍa's son Muda Gauḍa, and Bomma Deva Gauḍa's younger brother Tiraka Gauḍa. These mustering horse and foot, presented themselves before Vīraṇṇa Oḍeyar. And Tiraka Gauḍa then said:—" We are not breakers of the word we have given: Vīra Pratāpa Harihara Mahārāya's great minister Guṇḍapa Daṇḍanātha gave us the title of Champion over the Three Kings (*mūvara rāyara gaṇḍa*). So that this title shall be sung (in songs), in such a manner will I break and put down the Beḍar force." Thus saying Tiraka Gauḍa, taking sword and shield, broke and put down the hostile force, slew and knocked down the leaders, himself dying nobly in the fight.[113]

We hear little of the Beḍars in Vijayanagara history till the memorable battle of Rākṣasa-Taṅgaḍi. But in the first quarter of the sixteenth century, they ventured to attack Nañja Rāja, the founder of the principality of Nañjarāyapaṭṭaṇa (in Coorg, to the north of the Kaveri).[114] It was about this time that they established themselves at Piriyapaṭṭana and Tuṅga. How they were enticed into a marriage alliance and treacherously dealt with by the Jaina leaders Cangalarāya and Maṅgarasa, has been described by us in detail elsewhere.[115]

The Beḍars were not wholly reconciled to the generous principles which Kṛṣṇa Deva Rāya the Great had enunciated in his well known book *Āmukta-mālyada.* They continued to be an unruly element, although during the reign of that monarch and of his successors, they did not appear on the scene as they had done in the reign of Deva Rāya I. When, however, the combined armies of the Muhammadan kings of the Deccan slew the gallant old monarch Rāma Rāya on the battle-field of Rākṣasa Taṅgaḍi, in about A. D. 1565, the Beḍars got an opprtunity of doing incalculable harm to the famous Hindu city of Vijayanagara. They ransacked the treasures, plundered the defenceless people and completed the ruin of the great city. Even foreign witnesses noticed the depradations committed by the Beḍars whom they called Bedues.[116]

This great defeat which the Hindus suffered on the plain of Rākṣasa-Taṅgaḍi enabled the Beḍars to establish principalities of their own. The most powerful of these Beḍar states were those of Chitaldroog, Hoḷalkere, and Hiriyūr. The rulers of these principalities were Beḍars by caste but they claimed to be of the *Vālmikī-gotra* and *Kāmageṭi-vams'a.* Their *birudus* included those of *Mahānāyakācārya,* and *Kāmageṭi-kastūri.* This last was a distinctive prefix to their names.

That the Vijayanagara government itself gave them permission to assume some sort of independence after the battle of Rākṣasa-Taṅgaḍi, is clear from two epigraphs dated A. D. 1568 which give us the following details :— That in the reign of Sadās'iva Rāya, on the sudden death of Rāma Rāya Deva, the city, throne, and countries of the ruler being destroyed and in ruins, Tirumala Rājayya Deva Mahā-arasu, the brother of the famous Regent, granted the Hoḷalkere-sīme to Kāmageṭi Medakeri Nāyaka as an *amara-māgaṇi*; and that the latter made it over to his younger brother-in-law Gulliyappa Nāyaka as an *umbaḷi.* We may incidentally mention here that Kāmageṭi Kastūri Medakeri Nāyaka generously endowed (with grants of land) the temple of Gopāla Kṛṣṇa. The image of the god had been originally set up in former times by king Janamejaya, buried in the earth by the Hoysala king Viṣṇuvardhana Deva, recovered by Kṛṣṇa Deva, Rāya and Aḷiya Rāma Rājayya. Whether the image was an ancient one or not, the founder of the Beḍar principality of Chitaldroog had given ample proof of his high sense of duty towards the cause of the Hindu religion.[117]

The Chitaldroog chiefs continued to exercise power for more than 150 years. They extended their territory at the expense of the Sante Bennūr and the Harpanhaḷḷi chiefs. These latter, we may note, were

Beḍars themselves. The founder of the Beḍar principality of Harpanhaḷḷi, was one Dādayya. He set up a quasi-independent government at Harpanhaḷḷi, according to some, after the battle of Rākṣasa-Taṅgaḍi.[118]

To resume the history of the Chitaldroog chieftains, we find them waging constant wars with the Marāṭhas, the Moghuls, and the Keladi kings.[119] Keladi proved the ruin of Chitaldroog. Somas'ekhara Nāyaka II's scheme of aggrandizement soon brought within the Keladi kingdom Sīrā, Ajjampūr, Sante Bennūr, and other places which had been under the influence of the Moghuls. He soon turned his attention towards the Beḍars of Chitaldroog.

In A. D. 1748 was fought the decisive battle of Māyakoṇḍa in which Chitaldroog suffered a disastrous defeat, its ruler Medakeri Nāyaka being slain. An incident in this battle was of great importance in the history of the land. One of the allies of Chitaldroog was Candā Sāhīb. He was then just returning southwards from his place of captivity at Satāra. In the battle of Māyakoṇḍa he was taken prisoner, and his son was killed. While being led in triumph to Beḍnūr, he induced his Muhammadan guards to march with him to the French camp instead. He took Arcot in A. D. 1750,[120] and ushered thereby a new era in the struggle between the Anglo-French powers in India.

Keladi Somaśekhara Nāyaka II was an avowed enemy of the Beḍars. In A. D. 1758 he ordered the arrest of Manca Baramaṇa, who was committing lawlessness and causing grave trouble to the Keladi State. Koḍihaḷḷi Basa cut off the head of this Beḍar leader and soon put an end to the Beḍar trouble.[121]

But the final disappearance of Chitaldroog as a factor in the Karṇāṭaka history took place only in the reign of Haidar 'Ali. After a prolonged siege, he captured it in A. D. 1779 through the treachery of some Mussulman officers. It is said that Haidar 'Ali in order to break up the Beḍar population, whose patriotism had prolonged the siege for quite a long time, transported 20,000 Beḍars to Seringapatam where the choicest of them were formed into regular battalions of convert captives called Celas.[122]

The tradition of enlisting the Beḍars in royal service is to be traced to the Hoysala times when Vīra Ballāḷa III had under him Beḍar contingents commanded by General Narasiṅga. This great Hoysala ruler's stout enemy, Kumāara Kampila, as is related in Nañjuṇḍa's narrative *Paradāra Sodara Rāmana Kathe*, was a Beḍar himself. And he too had battalions of Beḍars under him in his struggle against the Hoysala king as well as in his wars against the Sultan of Delhi. Kumāra Kampila, we may incidentally observe, used to go out a-hunting with his Beḍar followers (*Śabara-kula*).[123]

There is every reason to believe that the Marāṭha armies too had Beḍar contingents in their vanguard, although some include them among robber classes. Manucci informs us that along with the army of the Marāṭhas, there "marched privileged and recognised thieves called Bederia (Bidari)" (*i. e.*, Beḍars), who were "the first to invade the enemy's territory" where they plundered every thing they found. The handsomest items were reserved for the general, the rest they sold on their own account.[124] It is opined by some that, according to a contemporary ballad, the Marāṭha generals employed a number of Beḍars exactly for the same purpose for which the professed Pendharis (Pindaris) were usually engaged, *viz.*, for sharing the spoils with the State.[125]

This custom seems to have prevailed also in the Mughul camp. We gather this also from Manucci who, in continuation of the above remarks, relates thus:—That Prince Shāh 'Ālam when he was within the territories of S'ivāji, near Goa, had in his army seven thousand such (Beḍars) whose orders were to ravage the lands of Bardes.[126]

It was not only as soldiers and kingdom builders that the Beḍars contributed to the history of the land. A few Beḍar names illumine the history of Hindu culture. The most celebrated name of a Beḍar author, as is well known, is that of of Vālmīki, to whom the *Rāmāyana* is ascribed. Another famous name is that of the great S'aiva saint Kaṇṇappa. This Beḍar of Appaduvūr which is also named Udūpuru, in the Kāḷahastigiri district, is also known as Kaṇṇappa-Nāyanār, Mukkaṇṇa, and Netrārpaka. It is said that Kaṇṇappa was a devotee of S'iva; and that in his own Beḍar way, he used to pluck flowers and leaves and put them first on his own head before he carried them as an offering to S'iva. The remains of savoury meat dishes were put by him in a cup of leaves and carried in his hand. He used to remove the flowers of the former day in his quaint manner—push them aside with his feet which had shoes on them. And for cleansing the image, he used his own spittle instead of water. Then he used to offer the meat to the god who, the tradition runs, ate it. Once to try his devotion, S'iva appaeared as if he was wounded in one eye. Kaṇṇappa seeing the wound on the face of the image, plucked out one of his eyes, and replaced the wounded eye of the god. Pleased with his devotion, S'iva is said to have given him three eyes.[127]

This great S'aiva saint is represented in sculptures in the Karṇāṭaka. The pillars of the front half of the Candramauḷīs'vara temple at Doḍḍa-Baḷḷāpura, contain a figure of Kaṇṇappa.[128] He is depicted as kicking a *liṅga* in the sculptures of the Bhimes'vara temple at Kaivāra.[29] In the sculptures of the Veṅkaṭaramaṇa temple at Cikkanāyakanahaḷḷi, we have an additional detail to the one mentioned at Kaivāra : Kaṇṇappa is piercing his eye with an arrow.[130] A third detail in addition to the two described in the Cikkanāyakanahaḷḷi temple is given in the sculptures of the Mallikārjuna temple at Paṅkajanhaḷḷi. Here we see him armed with a bow.[131]

Another well known Beḍar devotee is Kanaka Dāsa of Kāginele in the Dharwar district. Born about the year A. D. 1550, Kanaka soon left his native place and came to Uḍipi in Tuḷuva (mod. South Kanara). Here in the celebrated centre of Dvaitism, he was held to be the model of devotion by the religious heads of the eight *maṭhas* established by the great Madvācārya. Kanaka was a remarkable poet as well. Some of his works are *Narasimha Hastuva*, written in honour of the god at Kāginele, *Haribhaktisāra*, *Rāmadhyāna caritra*, and numerous other hymns, which are very popular all over the Vaiṣṇava world in the Karṇāṭaka and Tuḷuva.[132] Close to the Kṛṣṇa temple at Uḍipi is a little shrine of Kanaka where he used to pray to his favourite deity Kṛṣṇa. This shrine is held in high veneration by the people.

The Tamil land also contains an account of Beḍars who were instrumental in building a shrine. This we gather from the traditional account of Puṇḍi, which contains a Jaina *basadi*, in the Āṛṇī district. Two Beḍars named Irumban and Pandan came to the place where the temple now stands, in order to dig up an edible kind of root. An ascetic named Tellumaninā̄thar was doing penance there in a white ant hill. While digging the two hunters struck him in the breast with their implement. Being frightened at the mistake they had committed, they tried to rectify it by shading the ascetic with leaves and by bringing him daily offerings of fruits, flowers, honey, and roots. After some time another holy man named Samayanāthar came there. On seeing the newcomer, the Beḍars were frightened beyond words, but recovered their self-possession when he showed signs of favour. The newcomer was then conducted to the spot where Tellumaninā̄thar was doing penance; and at his instance, the Beḍars hastened to inform the king news of their discovery.

Now, the king, the tradition continues, was suffering from a great calamity. An evil spirit had possessed his sister, and it destroyed all who attempted to exorcize it. The king who is called in the account Rāyer, had promised to give half of his kingdom to any one who could cast it out. Pandan, the Beḍar, reminded the king of his promise; and as he was talking, the spirit quitted the body of the sister of the king. She came out dressed with a plate of flowers in her hand, and with this set out to the residence of the sage whose power had cured her. The Rāyer followed her with his family, and on coming to the place paid homage to the sage. The king then directed that the temple which had been left unfinished was to be completed. The two Beḍars were rewarded with grants of villages which came to be called after their names.[133] Since the title *Rāyer* is generally given in Tamil accounts to Kṛṣna Deva Rāya the Great, we may place the events mentioned above in the sixteenth century A. D.

CHAPTER V

MISCELLANEOUS TRIBES

Summary :— Pulindas – Das'ārṇas – Mātaṅgas – Puṇḍras – Lambakarṇas – Karṇapravarṇas – Ekapādas– Yakṣas – and Kinnaras.

THE PULINDAS

A tribe consanguineous to those mentioned in the previous pages were the Pulindas. We have noted how, according to the *Aitareya Brāhmaṇa*, the origin of the Pulindas was the same as that of the S'abaras and other wild tribes living on the borders of the Aryan territories. They are mentioned by Ptolemy as Pulindae or (Pulindai agnaphagoi).[1] The *Mahāvamso* has the following account of their origin:—In the story of the consecration of Vijaya, we are told that Vijaya had one son and one daughter by the Yakkhiṇī. The latter went to Laṅkāpura with the two children but being suspected (as a spy) she was killed by the Yakkhas. But her maternal uncle saw the two children and advised them to flee. With speed they fled to Sumantakūṭa (*i. e.*, Adam's Peak). The brother, the elder of the two, took his sister, the younger, for his wife, and multiplying with sons and daughters, they dwelt with the king's leave in Malaya (*i. e.*, the central mountain region in the interior of Ceylon). From these sprang the Pulinda. It is opined that Pulinda here is evidently a name of the Waeddās. The tract of country inland between Colombo, Kalatura, Galle, and the mountains is now called Sabaragamuva. This name is derived from S'abara, a synonym for Pulinda.[2] It is not improbable that the name Waeddā is itself a corruption of the term Beḍa.

The Pulindas are located in the middle and southern regions in the *Rāmāyaṇa* and the *Mahābhārata*. In the former they are said to occupy the middle portion of the Deccan.[3] Bhīma marched eastwards and then turning towards the south, entered the country of the Pulindas (in the south) and brought Sukmāra and Sumitra under his sway. Then he went to Cedi.[4] In the course of his southern conquests, Sahadeva came upon the Pulindas whom he conquered. After subjugating the mighty monarchs of the Nācinas and the Arvukas, and the various forest kings of that part of the country, Sahadeva reduced to subjection the king Vātādhipa. And defeating in battle the Pulindas, he fought for one day with the king Pandrya. Then he came to the celebrated caves of Kiṣkindhyā and here he fought for several days with the monkey kings Mainda and Dvividha.[5] In the topographical list of the *Bhīṣmu Parva*, the Sindhas, the Pulindas, the Uttamas, and a host of others are mentioned.[6]

It is evident from the above that there were branches of the Pulindas in the south as well as in the north. The southern branch seems to have extended eastwards. This is probably the reason why in the *Viṣṇu Purāṇa* the order given in the *Bhīṣma Purvá* is repeated, and the Bhojas, the Sindhas, the Pulindas, and the Uttamas together with other peoples are mentioned.[7] A further proof of their widespread domicile is given in the same *Purāṇa* which says that there were also the Vindhyacūlikas, the Pulindas, the Kalkalas, the Mālavas, the Mallavas, and others.[8]

The *Mārkaṇḍeya Purāṇa* and the *Garuḍa Purāṇa* place them in the south. The former locates them along with the S'abaras in the southern region; while the latter designates them together with Aṣmakas, Jimūtayanas, Kāmbojas, Karṇāṭas, and Ghatas as southerners.[9]

The Pulinda *janapada* is located in the north of Bharatavarṣa in the *Matsya Purāṇa.*[10] We are told in the same work that the abode of the Pulindas was watered by the Ganges which striking against the Vindhyas falls in the southern ocean. But the *Matsya Purāṇa* also calls the Pulinda country an Aryan *janapada,*[11] and classes it with the land of the Kirātas and the Vidhyādharas in the south.[12]

The *Pulinda-gaṇa* (tribe) is mentioned in the *Bṛhatsamhitā.*[13]

They were wrongly supposed to have been mentioned in the Rock Edicts of Aśoka.[14] But, as Hultzsch pointed out, the term occurring in the Rock Edicts was *Palida, Pālada,* and *Pāriṇḍa,*[15] thus bringing to our notice a new people about whom nothing is known for the present.

We have seen above how the Pulindas together with the S'abaras are mentioned by Kauṭalya in his *Arthas'āstra.*

The Pulindas of the southern regions have not been insignificant in the history of the country. In the historical narrative called *Paradāra Sodara Rāmana Kathe* by Nañjuṇḍa, we are told that Rāma Deva of Devagiri had four sons, one of whom married a Pulinda woman. He was, therefore, declared an outcaste. When the Turuṣkas captured Devagiri, this excommunicated prince sought service under the chief of Citrakūṭadurga, who entrusted him with the duty of defending the frontier of his principality. In the family of this outcaste prince was born Mummuḍi Siṅgha, whose son was Kumāra Kaṁpila, the hero of the narrative.[16] Kumāra Kaṁpila is called in the same work king of Pulinda.[17]

In the *Cennabasava Purāṇa* written by the poet Virūpākṣa Paṇḍita in A. D. 1585, the Pulinda kingdom is included among the fifty-six countries (*cchappanna-des'a or s'aṭ–pañcā–s'aṭ vis'aya*) into which India was conventionally divided.[18] In the Tamil geography too mention is made of the fifty-six divisions among which the Pulinda kingdom is included.[19]

The Pulindas were, therefore, familiar to the people of the Karṇāṭaka. Poet Sālva (circa A. D. 1550) thus describes their women :—

Created by Brahmā with the forms from the pith of the darkness of the rainy season (or the dark fortnight), with light in their eyes which the Creator had infused into them from the lightning of the rainy season soon after having washed (or polished) the woods by the drops of rain–, the coquettish (and charming) Pulinda women shone in company of the female dwellers :

Kār-iruḷa kattaleya tiruḷim vāri-ruha-bhavana-olidu nirmisi |
nāriyara rūhaṅgaḷan-añjanarūañjadi puṭaviṭṭu ||
kāra miñcumaṃ-avara kaṇnoḷu serisidan-ene gāḍiyaru kān- |
tāracariyaru meredar-alli Pulindara-ogginalli[20] ||

THE NIṢĀDAS

A prominent section of the wild tribes were the Niṣādas whose name has so often figured in the previous pages. The origin of the Niṣādas, according to Manu, is traced to the admixture of castes. The offspring of a Brāhmaṇa father and a S'ūdra mother was a Niṣāda. The son of a Niṣāda by a S'ūdra female was a Pukkasa; but the son of a S'ūdra by a Niṣāda female became a Kukkuṭaka. The Niṣādas, as Manu enjoins, were to kill and collect fish for other people.[21] The *Garuḍa Purāṇa*, however, has an ingenious explanation to give concerning the origin of the Niṣādas. It relates that Aṅga's son was Vena who was an atheist and an irreligious man. This perpetrator of iniquities was killed by the *ṛṣis* with Kus'a. They then churned his thigh for a son and thereat sprang up a son, greatly dwarfish and black. They then said:— " Sit down, sit down ! ", and he was called Niṣāda dwelling on the mount Vindhya.

The same *Purāṇa* informs us of the habitat of the Niṣādas. It relates that the S'trīrājyas, the Saindhavas, the Mlecchas, the godless Yavanas together with the Niṣādas and the people of Mathura inhabited the western countries.[22]

The western home of the Niṣādas as given in the *Garuḍa Purāṇa* is borne out in some manner by the statements in the *Harivaṃśa* which places the Niṣādas in the west as well as in the east. It describes Niṣāda a the son of Atithi who was the grandson of Rāma. The son of Niṣāda was Naḷa whose son was Nabha. Devaṣrava's son Ēkalavya, we are told in the same work, was brought up by the Niṣādas, and was accordingly called Naiśadhi. But, in another context, the author of the *Harivaṁśa* describes the Niṣādas as collecting jewels born in water in small and big boats, in the sea belonging to the province of Vanavāsi.[23] Since the Vanavāsa kingdom was situated on the western side of India, we have to surmise that the Niṣādas spoken of here lived also on the western coast of India.

We have already noted the existence of a Niṣāḍa kingdom in the times of the *Mahābhārata*. The earliest historical reference to a principality of the Niṣādas on the western side of India is in the Jūnāgadh inscription of the Mahākṣātrapa Rudradāman, dated in the 72nd year (circa A. D. 150). In this record Rudradāman is said to have brought under his sway the Niṣāda country along with eastern and western Mālwā, the region round Dwārkā, etc.[24]

Of greater prominence was the Niṣāda province in the east. The antiquity of this Niṣāda kingdom mentioned in the *Brahmāṇḍa Purāṇa* as having been one of the provinces ruled over by the Guptas, has been traced to the times of Naḷa. And it has been located in the vicinity of Berar, if not in Berar itself.[25]

Mention has been already made of the existence of a Niṣāda ruler so late as the eighth century A. D.

With the evidence of the epics and the *Purāṇas* before us, credit may be given to the assertion of the Kannaḍa writer Nijaguṇayogi who includes the Niṣāda principality among the different kingdoms of India.[26]

Buddhist literature contains many details concerning the Niṣādas. The *Cchadanta Jātaka*, for example gives us an interesting portraiture of the Niṣādas whom it calls Luddhakas. It was when Culla Subhaddā caused all the Luddhakas of Benares to be summoned by her husband, to get a pair of tusks of the elephant Cchadanta (the Boddhisatta) in order to satisfy an old grudge she bore him. The 60,000 Luddhakas of Benares presented themselves; and all except one expressed their inability to secure the pair of tusks. This particular hunter called Soṇuttara is thus described:—He was broad-footed, with a calf (thigh?) swollen like an alms-basket, big ribbed, thick bearded, with copper coloured teeth, with disgustingly (prominently ?) red eyes (or with scars disfiguring his face), ill-shaped, and revolting to the sight :—

patthaṭa-pādam bhatta-puṭa-sadisa-janghaṃ mahā-jānum mahā-phāsukaṃ bahala-massuṃ tāmba-dāṭhikaṃ nibbiddha-piṅgalaṃ dussanṭhānam bhibhaccham....Soṇuttaram nāma Nesādam...

In a long and interesting passage in the same *Jātaka*, we are told how Soṇuttara armed himself for seven days before he reached the summit of Suvaṇṇapassa. A sharp knife, a hatchet (axe), a spade, a *nikhādana* (a sharp instrument), *muṭṭika* (a sort of a hammer ?), a dagger, a grass cutter, an instrument for cutting bamboos and thickets, a sword, an iron staff, a stake, a three-pronged iron fork, a bag of leather, a leather sack, a bag to hold a hog's-head's weight (?), leather ropes and straps, shoes big enough for elephant's foot, a leather parachute, wood (flint ?) for kindling fire, an outfit, a bag of cakes, a ladder, a dry plank, a trough-shaped canoe, and a quiver–with these and other things necessary for the journey, Soṇuttara crossed the mountain.[27]

THE DAS'ĀRNAS

According to the Greek geographers, the land of the Daśārṇas was almost next to that of the Kirātas. In the ***Periplus Mari Erythrae*** ships sailing northwards from Dōsārene arrived at the land of the wild flat nosed Kirradai who, like the other wild tribes, were supposed by Lassen to be man-eaters.[28] McCrindle identified the land of the Dōsārene with the country on both sides of the Vaitaraṇī.

Ptolemy locates the Daśārṇas in the Gangetic valley after the Minagara and before the Kokala.

He describes the mouth of the Dosaron. McCrindle commented on the above by saying that the Dosaron was the river of the people mentioned in the *Viṣṇu Purāṇa*-whom we shall presently describe-as belonging to the south-east of the Madhya-deśa in juxtaposition with the S'abaras or Suars. He also derived the word from *das'an* (ten) and *ṛṇa* (fort), meaning thereby the land of ten forts.[29]

Gerini identifying the Ts'wan, T'wan, or Doan tribes of Eastern Yünnan with Ptolemy's Doānai, remarked that in the Greek geographer's time, a conspicuous part of these people (the Das'ārṇas) had already advanced into Eastern Lāos or Das'ārṇa which they held under sway.

Gerini explains how the names Das'ārṇa and Mālwā were transported to northern Siam. The region of the Eastern or Whifte bellied Lāu-which Gerini describes in detail-was known to Ptolemy as the country of the Doānai, a people lying, according to the same geographer, along the river of the same name. Previous to this designation being applied, however, or soon after its origin, the country of the Lāu was classically known as Mālavades'a or Mālwā-a name which it retained till recent times under the corrupt forms of Malā, Mālā, Mālavā. As the term Mālavā collectively applied to the whole region of Lāos was imported from central India, where it designated the country known as Mālwā, so was the term Das'ārṇa also introduced from the same quarter. And as there it denoted the eastern part of Mālwā, so by analogy it was given in Further India to the corresponding portion of the Indo-Chinese Mālavā, *i. e.*, Eastern Lāos. The term Das'ārṇa thus became identified with Ptolemy's Dasana.[30]

Hindu literature contains notices of the Das'ārṇa country and its people. The *Rāmāyaṇa* locates the Das'ārṇa city in the south :—

Tato-Godāvarīm-ramyām-Kṛṣṇaveṇim-Mahānadīm ।
Mekalām-Utkalān-ca-eva-Das'ārṇa-nagarāṇi-api ॥ [31]

Relying on the strength of the above verse, Sewell placed the Das'ārṇas in the country south of the Tuṅgabhadrā.[32]

But in the times of the *Mahābhārata*, we find the Daśārṇas spread to the west and east. Surrounding the kingdom of the Kurus, we are told, were many countries beautiful and abounding in corn. These were Pāncāla, Cedi, Matsya, Sūrasena, Pattacara, Daśārṇa, Navarāṣṭra, S'ālva, Yughandhara, Surāṣṭra, Avanti, and the spacious Kuntīrāṣṭra.[33]

The conquests of Nakula enable us to determine better the location of the Daśārṇas and their country. He was bent on conquering the west. After subjugating the (people of the) mountain called Rohitaka that was dear unto the famous Kārttikeya, the Mattamayūrakas, the whole of the desert country called Ṣairiṣaka, and the Mahettha, he encountered the royal sage Akroṣa. He then conquered the Daśārṇas, the S'ivis, the Trigartas, the Amvaṣtas, the Mālavas, the five tribes of the Karṇāṭakas, and those twice-born classes called Madhamākhyas and Vātadhānas.[34]

But at the same time the Daśārṇas were found in the east. In the course of his eastern conquests, Bhīma entered the country of the Pāncālas, then vanquished the Gandhakas, the Videhas, and then subjugated the Daśārṇas. There in the country of the Daśārṇas, the king called Sudharma with bare arms did fierce battle with Bhīma who, beholding that feat of the illustrious Daśārṇa king, appointed him as the first in command of his forces. Perhaps it was this mighty ruler of the Daśārṇas who was placed, together with the king of the Prayāgas, the Dāserakas, the Anūpakas, and the Kirātas, in the neck of the *krauñcāruṇa* array formed by Yudhiṣṭira on the occasion of that memorable battle.

The topographical list in the same (*Bhīsma*) *Parva* mentions the Uttamas, the Daśārṇas, the Mekalas, the Utkalas, and others; and again the Jātharas, the Kukurus, and the Daśārṇas,[35] thus confirming the association of the Daśārṇas with the Mekalas and the Utkalas as given in the *Rāmāyaṇa*.

The *Viṣṇu Purāṇa* follows both the epics in its location of the Daśārṇas. It enumerates the peoples in the following order:—the Bhojas, the Sindhu Pulindas, the Uttamas, the Daśārṇas, the Mekals, the Pāñcālas, and the others. Then, again, the same *Purāṇa* relates thus— the Madrabhujingas, the Kāśis, the Aparakāśis, the Jātharas, the Kukurus, the Daśārṇas, the Kuntis, and the Avantis. In a later passage we are told that there were Kulindāpatyakas, Vātāyanas, Daśārṇas, Romanas, Kuśavindus, and others.[36]

The *Mārkaṇḍeya Purāṇa* mentions the Daśārṇa river after the Mandākini and before the Citrakūta. The same work classes the Daśārṇa people among the inhabitants living on the slopes of the Vindhyas along with the Sarajas, the Karuṣas, the Keraḷas, the Utkalas, the Uttamarṇas, the Bhojas, and the Kiṣkindhakas.

The eastern home of the Daśarṇas is suggested in the same *Purāṇa* which places the Daśārṇa country between the Kaṭakasthaḷas (identified by Pargiter with Cuttack), and the unidentified naked Hārikas-countries said to be situated in the Tortoise's right fore-foot.[37]

Elephants of the Daśārṇa and western countries, as is related in Kauṭalya's *Arthas'āstra*, were of middle quality, while those bred in Kaliṅga, Aṅga, and Karūśa and in the east were the best, and those of Saurāṣṭra and Pañca-jana (republican tribes?) were of low quality.[38]

In the *Matsya Purāṇa* we have the Daśārṇa country placed on the western extremity of the Vindhyācala in the following order:— Mālawā, Karūśa, Mekāla, Utkala, Auṇḍra, Māsa, Daśārṇa, Bhoja, etc. But in an earlier passage in the same work, we are told that the Mlecchas and the Aryans reside in Bharatavarṣa mingling with each other without distinction; and that they drink the waters of many rivers such as the Ganges, the Sindhu, the Sarasvatī, the Mandākinī, the Daśārṇa, the Citrkūṭa, the Tāmasā, etc.[39] Thus the statement given in the *Matsya Purāṇa* as regards the location of the Daśārṇa river is in conformity with that given in the *Mārkaṇḍeya Purāṇa*.

A Daśārṇa province is mentioned in the *Harivaṃs'a*. That same work informs us that among the allies of Jarāsandha was a king of Daśārṇa.[40]

We have already cited the evidence from the *Bṛhatsaṃhitā* in regard to the south-eastern home of the Niṣādas, the Purikas, the Daśārṇas, and others, while dealing with the S'abaras. The *Bṛhatsaṃhitā*, we may be permitted to say, calls the people in question Dās'ārṇa.[41]

In the section on the *Purva-Megha* in his *Meghadūta*, Kālidāsa depicts a love-sick Yakṣa and makes him address the following to the Cloud:— When you will be in the vicinity, the Das'ārṇa country will have the hedges of its gardens white coloured with the *ketaka* flowers opened at their apexes, the sacred trees of its villages will be greatly disturbed by the nest-making of the domestic birds, its skirts of Jaṁbu forests dark with their ripe fruit, and the swans halting there for some days.[42]

Kālidāsa gives us the most decisive hint as regards the exact location of Das'ārṇa in the next verse which says the following:—On reaching its capital bearing the name Vidis'ā famed in all the quarters, you (Cloud) will at once obtain the entire fruit of your love, since you will drink the sweet water with its undulating ripples of Vetravatī, like its face full of the knitting of eyebrows, in a manner charming on account of your thundering on the border of its bank.[43]

The poet gives us one more detail which may be noted before we locate the Daśārṇa country in the north. The Yakṣa continues to address the Cloud:—Though the road will be circuitous to you, set out for the north, do not be averse to contract the acquaintance of the upper vault of mansions of Ujjainī; and if you will not be delighted there with the eyes of the women of the town, with their outer corners tremulous and dazzled by the flashes of the streaks of lightning, you will be deceived (*i. e.*, you will have missed the fruit of existence).[44]

Kālidāsa's invaluable testimony helps us to locate with some precision the Daśārṇa country. Its capital was Vidiśā on the river Vetravatī, the modern Betwa (which rises near Bhopal and flows into the Jumnā), a little way east of Ujjain. Vidiśā has been identified by Cunningham with the modern Bhilsa, or rather with Besnagar, the ancient capital which is close to Bhilsa.[45] The river Daṣārṇa which has been placed between the Mandākinī and Citrakūṭa, is the modern Das'an between the Betwa and the Ken, the latter being a tributary on the right bank of the Jumnā.[46]

According to Wilson the people of the Daśārṇa country were those of the ten forts subsequently multiplied into thirty-six, such being the meaning of Cchattisgaṛh which seems to be the site of Daśārṇa.[47] The basis for this is perhaps to be found in the *S'abdakalpadruma* which defines Das'ārṇa as the land of the ten forts or of ten waterways—*Daśārṇaḥ (daśarṇāni) durga-bhūmayo jalā-ghāra-va yatra*...Here too, following the authority of the *Bṛhatsaṃhitā*, the Das'ārṇa country is located in the south-east of the Vindhya mountain.[48]

It was evidently the ruler of this Daśārṇa country who is referred to in an inscription dated A. D. 1068 which describes the suzerainty of the Western Cālukya monarch Trailokyamalla Āhavamalla Deva thus :- The worthless kings of Lāṭa, Kaliṅga, Gaṅga, Karahāṭa, Turuṣka, Varāḷa, Coḷa, Karṇāta, Surāṣṭra, Māḷava, Das'ārṇa, Kos'ala, Keraḷa, and other countries did not remain insolent but gave tribute and stopped within their appointed boundaries.[49]

The *Sāḷuvābhyudayam* which, as we have already seen, mentions a S'abarendra chief as having been conquered by Sāḷuva Nṛsiṁha, also speaks of that king having subjugated a country called Das'ārṇa. This statement was also incorrectly interpreted by Dr. S. Krishnswami Aiyangar to mean the conventional invasion by that monarch.[50] Although we are unable for the present to identify the ruler of the Das'ārṇa country who was conqured by Sāḷuva Nṛsiṁha, yet there cannot be any doubt that the victory mentioned in the *Sāḷuvābhyudayam* was a real one. In the present state of our knowledge we find it difficult to identify the Das'ārṇa country of the *Sāḷuvābhyudayam* with that near Mālwā, since its conquest would have meant the subjugation of some of the Muhammadan Sultans who had by this time established themselves firmly to the north of Sāḷuva Nṛisiṁha's territory. We have, therefore, to surmise that the Das'ārṇa ruler whom the Vijayanagara ruler subdued must have belonged to the Das'ārṇa stock of the Tungabhadrā region. It was because this Das'ārṇa ruler was a tribal leader that his name may have been omitted in the poem.

THE MĀTAṄGAS

The Tungabhadrā basin is also associated with the name of another tribe which has left a celebrated name behind it. We refer to the Mātaṅgas whose modern representatives are called Māngs of the Bombay Presidency.[51] The *Rāmāyaṇa* enables us to locate the region of the Mātaṅgas. Kabandhaka relates to Rāma that near Paṁpā was an empty hermitage and that the Ṛiṣi Mātaṅga's forest was there. And the S'ramaṇa S'avari (S'abari), whom we have already introduced in an earlier connection, gives the following description of the forest :— See the charming great forest, she says to Rāma and Lakṣmaṇa, abounding in flowers and fruits, resembling a bank of clouds, filled with all sorts of deer and birds. This, she continues, is famous on earth as Mātaṅga's forest :—

S'avarī dars'ayāmāsa tāv-ubhau tad-vanam mahat ।
uvāca vacanaṃ ca-idaṃ tāv-ubhau Rāma-Lakṣmaṇau ॥
bahu-puṣpaphalaṃ ramyaṃ dars'aniyaṃ mahat vanaṃ ।
pas'ya megha-caya-prakhyaṃ-mṛga-pakṣi-gaṇa-ayutaṃ ।
Mātaṅga-vanaṃ-iti-etad-vis'rutaṃ bhuvi Rāghava[52] ॥

According to Pargiter, the Mātaṅga forest is represented by the stretch of country from Sholāpur to Poona, west of the Riṣyamūkha range.[53]

The *Mahābhārata* contains an account of the Mātaṅga *tīrtha.* We are told that after going from Gayā, one reaches Dharmapriṣṭha. There dwelleth Dharma for ever. Drinking the water of a well which is there, and purifying one's self by a bath, he that offers oblations to the gods and the *pitṛis* is cleansed of all his sins, and ascends to heaven. There in that *tirtha* is another of the great Riṣi Mātaṅga of high soul under complete control.[54]

It is in all likelihood this Mātaṅga *tīrtha* which is described in the *Matsya Purāna* to have been in the east.[55]

We shall presently see that Mātaṅga was also the name given to a centre where diamonds were found. This is related in a work called *Ratnaparīkṣa* by Buddhabhaṭṭa. The *Bṛhatsamhitā* also mentions Mātaṅga as a diamond centre.[56]

In Buddhist literature too the name Mātaṅga has become famous. The *Mātaṅga Jātaka* relates that when Brahmadatta was the king of Benares, the Great Being was born outside the city as a Cāṇḍāla's son, and that they gave him the name of Mātaṅga, the Elephant. Afterwards he attained wisdom, and his fame was blown abroad as the wise Mātaṅga.[57]

It is related in the *Cariyapīṭika* how the Boddhisatta was born as a Jaṭila under the name of Mātaṅga. He was noted for his severe penance and piety. He lived along with a Brāhmaṇa on the bank of the Ganges. But the hermitage of Mātaṅga was above, that of the Brāhmaṇa, below. Once while walking along the bank of the river, the two met face to face. And the Brāhmaṇa out of envy cursed that the head of

Mātaṅga should be broken. More in order to save his own *sīla* (character) than his head, Mātaṅga, although capable of reverting the curse on the Brāhmaṇa himself, yet allowed it to take effect.[58]

Both in early Buddhist and Hindu literature, therefore, the name Mātaṅga has been deified. It is interesting to observe how it has also been associated with the fate of a prince in Kālidāsa's work. The elephant which emerged from the Narmadā and which confronted Aja, told him how its name was Priyamvada, son of Priyadars'ana, king of the Gandharvas, and how it had been transformed into an elephant in consequence of the curse of the sage Mātaṅga brought about by its own arrogance.[59]

Bāṇa gives a sketch of a Mātanga thus in his *Kādambarī*:—King S'ūdraka was told that a Cāṇḍālī maiden with a parrot was waiting to see him. She came in. Before her went a man whose hair was hoary with age, whose eyes were of the colour of the red lotus, whose joints, despite the loss of youth, were firm from incessant labour, whose form though that of a Mātaṅga, was not to be despised, and who wore a white raiment meet for a court. Behind her went a Cāṇḍāla boy, with locks falling on either shoulder, bearing a cage.[60]

One of the sons of the Brāhmaṇa renegades who had turned into Kirātas in the Vindhyan regions, as we already noticed in Daṇḍin's *Das'akumāracarita*, was Mātaṅga.[61]

The Mātaṅgas as an historical factor appear in the inscriptions of the Western Cālukyas, the Hoysalas, and the Coḷas. The Aihole inscription of the Western Cālukya king Pulikes'in II, dated A. D. 634-35, informs us that Maṅgales'a, the younger brother of king Kīrtivarma, who picketed his horse on the shores of the east and west and covered all the points of the compass through the dust of his armies, became king. Having with hundreds of scintillating torches which were his swords, dispelled the darkness which was the race of the Mātaṅgas, in the bridal field of battle he obtained as his wife the lovely woman who was the goddess of (fortune of) the Kaṭacuriyas. The same record mentions Maṅgales'a's conquest of Revatī-dvīpa and the Mātaṅgas.[62] We may not be wrong in assuming that in the first quarter of the seventh century A. D., the Mātaṅgas had extended as far as the Revatī island, the identification of which, it must be confessed, is not yet a settled question.

But there cannot be any doubt that Revatī-dvīpa was conquered by Maṅgales'a. So late as A. D. 1123, an inscription relates that Maṅgales'a plundered (and conquered) that island.[63] Fleet, while editing the Aihole inscription given above, remarked that the Revatī island was an unknown locality.[64] In the same connection he remarked that Raivata was a patronymic of Kakuḍmi, the ruler of Anarta in Gujarat; and that Revatī being another name of mount Gīrnār, Revatī-dvīpa was perhaps the peninsula of Gujarat.[65] If this could be accepted, we could have maintained that the Mātaṅgas had extended as far as Girnar. But Fleet himself has identified the Narmadā with Revā.[66]

That the Narmadā was called Revā is proved by Daṇḍin who connects the licentious activities of Pracaṇḍavarman at Māhiṣmatī with Revā.[67] The close association of Revatī-dvīpa with Māhiṣmatī in the *Das'akumāracarita*; the defeat of the Kaḷacuriyas being coupled with that of the conquest of Revatī-dvīpa in the above quoted Aihole inscription of

Pulikeśin II; and the fact of Māhiṣmatī being an island in the Narmadā–as Fleet himself has told us–,[68] all these suggest conclusively that Revatī–dvīpa was no other than Māhiṣmatī itself, the famous capital of Kārtavīrya or Sahasrabāhu-Arjuna, from whom the Kaḷacuriyas claimed descent.[69]

For our purpose we may note that the coupling of the conquest of the Mātaṅgas with that of the island Revatī and of the Kaḷacuriyas leads us to the inevitable conclusion that the Mātaṅgas had not only spread themselves in the seventh century to the Narmadā but were also the allies of the Kaḷacuriyas, one branch of whom had settled in the Narmadā basin.[70]

The stronghold of the Mātaṅgas in the twelfth century was the Mātaṅga Hill. In about A. D. 1190 Ballāḷa Deva II is said to have captured Virāṭa-rāja's city, Kurugoḍu, the Mātaṅga Hill and other strategical points.[71] This Mātaṅga Hill could have been no other than the Mātaṅga Parvata which formed one of the five hills enclosing the city of Vijayanagara. The temple which can be seen to this day on its top was, as we shall presently narrate, the endowment of a famous Vijayanagara general.

An inscription dated A. D. 1228 supplies us with interesting details concerning the exact location of the hermitage of the Ṛṣi Mātaṅga. The epigraph praises the virtue of a Boyi woman named Dharaṇī Boyi. She was equal to Draupadī or Sītā. Spreading reed grass on the ground, and placing it together, she obtained a *moṟa* (or winnowing basket) in the middle of the Tuṅgabhadrā. Thus, in the shed which was the Mātaṅga Ṛṣi's *āśrama*, the Bova named Vanarāja Rāma and Dharaṇi Boyiti, making a pandal with reed grass, dwelt there for some time with devotion to S'īva, in complete satisfaction. When the period for the Tuṅgabhadrā, which is born from Brahmā's *kalas'a*, to come in the northern channel and the nine months (for the woman) had expired, and it was the time for her delivery, they saw the Tuṅgabhadrā coming down overflowing its banks; on which he placed that *moṛa* in the middle, and seeing that the devoted wife had borne a child, the Tuṅgabhadrā divided and flowed on.[72]

If this inscription can be given any credence, then, the hermitage of Ṛṣi Mātaṅga which is mentioned in it was evidently the place where the same empty hermitage of Mātaṅga had stood, which, as we remarked above, Kabandhaka had pointed out to Rāma as being near Paṁpā.

The Mātaṅgas, who must have occupied the region around Paṁpā in greater numbers than we can gather, are also mentioned in the history of the Tamil rulers. It is related in a record dated A. D. 1292 that in the solar race and Ina-vaṁs'a was born Karikāla Coḷa. And in his line was born king Maṅgi who, by his destruction of the elephants his enemies gained the name of Destroyer of the Mātaṅgas.[73] It cannot be made out whether there is any reference here to the association of the name Mātaṅga with an elephant which we have described above, or whether it points out to any stronghold of the Mātangas in the Tamil country in the thirteenth century.

The annals of Kiṣkindhyā region deal with the remarkable deeds of a brave Mātaṅga woman leader. This is narrated in Nañjuṇḍa's *Paradāra Sodara Rāmana Kathe* mentioned above in connection with Kumāra Rāma of Kaṁpila. The events described in this narrative may be assigned to the latter part of the thirteenth and the beginning of the fourteenth centuries of the Christian era. On Nemi Malluka, the general of the Delhi Sultan, being defeated by Rāmanātha of Kampila, the Sultan rebuked his general and angrily ordered the capture of Rāmanātha. But none dared to undertake the responsibility of meeting Rāmanātha. Only a woman named Mātaṅga volunteered her services. She was born in the Mātaṅga caste and was the door-keeper of the Sultan. The Sultan being pleased with her words, presented her with a famous flag-staff called the "Ornament of the Three Worlds", and jewels, and appointed her commander-in-chief of an army of 12,000 elephants, 6000 camels, 1,00,000 horse, and 10,000,000 foot. Mātaṅgi led this huge army through many centres of strife and finally encamped at Bidire. And thence moved on to Kummaṭa, the citadel of Rāmanātha. Riding on an elephant she charged Rāmanātha, while Madhura Khan besieged Kummaṭa. The great fortress fell into the enemy's hands, Rāmanātha was killed, and Mātaṅgi took his head to Delhi, wrapped in a cloth of gold.[74]

The Mātaṅga Hill which we referred to above is one of the five famous hills which are said to have guarded the city of Vijayanagara, the others being Hemakūṭa, Basavas'riṅga, Mālyavanta and Kiṣkindhā.[75] An inscription dated A. D. 1347 informs us that Mādhava, the minister of Mārapa, one of the founders of Vijayanagara, built the S'iva temple on its top.[76]

Why Deva Rāya II is called in S'aka 1351 (A. D. 1429-30) *Mātaṅga Rāja*, as is related in a record of that date, we are unable to find out.[77] It is not improbable that there were some Mātaṅgas who were still powerful in the Kiṣkindhyā region.

Minister Mādhava's having built a S'iva temple

on the top of the Mātaṅga Parvata at Hampe, as given above, was not the only example of people associating the name of the famous Mātaṅga Ṛṣi with the worship of S'iva. In Satyaveḍu, twenty-three miles north of Tiruvaḷḷūr, in the Chingleput district, is an old S'iva temple which is said to have been built by Mātaṅga Maharṣi himself.[78]

Goddess Mātaṅgi and her son Pātappa have a shrine at Chikkanāyakanahaḷḷi in Mysore.[79] With the inclusion of Mātaṅgi as one of the *Mahāvidyās*, the deification of the Mātaṅgas in the Hindu religion is complete.[80]

THE PUṆḌRAS

Buddhabhaṭṭa gives in his *Ratnaparīkṣā*, a work which has been incorporated in the *pūrva-kaṇḍa* of the *Garuḍa Purāṇa*, as we narrated while describing the Mātaṅgas, the names of eight diamond centres, *viz.*, Surāṣṭra, Haima, Mātaṅga, Puṇḍra, Kaliṅga, Kośala the Vaiṇyā river and Sūrpāra.[81] Of these we are concerned here only with the Puṇḍras the Pauṇḍras, the Pauṇḍrikas, or the Puṇḍrakas, as they were also called. We have seen above how they have been so often mentioned along with the other wild tribes, in the digests of Hindu law-givers as well as in the epics. The Puṇḍrakas or Pauṇḍrakas were the people of western (and eastern) Bengal. According to Wilson, the following districts of Bengal and Bihar comprised the ancient Puṇḍra kingdom, *viz.*, Rājshāhi, Dinājpur, Rangpūr, Nadiyā, Bīrbhūm, Bardwān, Midnāpur, Jangal Mahāls, Rāmgaḍh, Pāchete, Palamow and part of Chunar.[82]

On the word Puṇḍra, Ranglal Banerjee remarked long ago thus :- That that word signified sugar cane of a particular species called *pauri-akh* in Bengali. Puṇḍra, therefore, meant the country of sugar cane. Now, the other name of Bengal-*Gauḍa*-is derived from *guḍa* or molasses, meaning thereby the country of the molasses. Hence the two names of Bengal-*Puṇḍra and Gauḍa*-have a similar meaning.[83]

With this identification of the country of the Puṇḍras, we may proceed to give a few references, especially to their relations with the kings of southern and western India. We shall not enter into the question of the Puṇḍrakas of ancient Bengal, since it has been so ably dealt with by Dr. Bimala Churn Law recently.[84] Notwithstanding the fact of the rulers of Vaṅga, Kaḷiṅga, Puṇḍra, and Suhma being described in the *Mahābhārata* to be the sons of Bali, the king of the eastern regions,[85] it is permissible to ask whether they were originally of the stock to which the other wild tribes belonged, or whether they "were not a barbarous nation," as Pargiter contended in his notices of the Puṇḍras occurring in the same epic. Further, we may also question the validity of his assertion whether they were to be placed only in the eastern regions and not in the south.[86]

As regards the former question, we have to recount here the opinion of Manu substantiated by the explanation given in the *Mahāhbārata*, concerning the degradation of certain races from the position of Kṣatriyas to that of S'ūdras, which we cited while dealing with the Kirātas. Whatever may be the importance to which the Puṇḍras rose in later history, there seems to be hardly any doubt that, according to classical opinion, they formed a branch of the larger group of the wild tribes, the most prominent of whom have figured in these pages. Like the Āndhras, whose history we have deliberately abstained from giving here, the Puṇḍras were a barbarous race to start with, and like them they too rose to great eminence as nation-builders in later history.

A further hint as regards the barbarous origin of the Puṇḍras is to be found in the statement of the *Mārkaṇḍeya Purāṇa* which locates them along with Kevalas and Golāngūlas (the cow-tailed people) in the south. Far from being erroneous, as Pargiter remarked,[87] there is reason to believe that a branch of the Puṇḍras–the greater part of whom had no doubt made Bengal their home–had moved southwards much in the same way the other tribes had done, in the early centuries of the Christian era. That the Puṇḍras were living near the Golāngūla tribe is further proved by the statement in the *Bṛhatsamhitā* which, while locating them in the eastern regions,[88] also speaks of the *Pauṇḍra Golāṅgūlah-Śrīparvata–Vardhamānāh-ca*[89]

It is these Puṇḍras who had migrated to the southern tracts and established themselves somewhere in the forests of the Āndhra and Kaliṅga kingdoms, that are obviously referred to in the epigraphs of the southern and western rulers. The Gaṅga king Satyavākya Koṅguṇivarma (I), who had Rājamalla as his first name, is praised thus in the Kūḍlūr plates of king Mārasiṁha assigned to A. D. 780:—"...the Vaṅga, the Puṇḍra, the Maghada and Kośala kings, and these the Kaliṅga, Āndhra, Dramiḷa kings with their allies, that were pierced by the weapons discharged by this king–thus did the people praise his valour in the Samiya battle." [90] That the victory which Rājamalla Satyavāka had won over the Puṇḍras was true is confirmed by a later record of Rājamalla II assigned to A. D. 904, which relates that the Puṇḍras were pierced in battle by the former.[91]

One of the Noḷambavāḍi rulers is also credited with a victory over the Puṇḍras. This was the great Vīra Pāṇḍya Deva, who received the name of Jagadekamalla from his overlord, the Western Cāḷukya king Jagadekamalla (II) Permma (A. D. 1138-1150). Vīra Pāṇḍya made mighty kings like those of Gaṅga, Kos'ala, Puṇḍra, Pārasi, Koṅgaṇa (Koṅkaṇa), and others tremble. This is related in a record dated A. D. 1148.[92]

Among the Hoysala monarchs there was one whose designs of aggrandizement included the subjugation of the Puṇḍras. An inscription dated A. D. 1169 informs us that among the kings who trembled before Hoysala monarch Narasiṁha I were the Puṇḍra and Āndhra rulers.[93]

THE LAMBAKARNAS, THE KARNAPRAVARNAS, AND THE ĒKAPĀDAS

We now come to certain tribes which have also to some extent contributed to the history of the land. These are the Laṃbakarṇas, the Karṇapravarṇas, and the Ēkapādas. It is true that we cannot for the present establish the identity between these and the tribes we have already described; but at the same time it must be confessed that we cannot pass over these races in silence, since they have moulded the destiny of some parts of India to an appreciable extent.

The existence of these peculiar tribes is vouchsafed for by Pliny who writes thus:—"In other places again (in India), there are men born with long hairy tails, and of remarkable swiftness of foot, while there are others that have ears so large as to cover the whole body."[94] These last were the Laṃbakarṇas of ancient India.

In no region of India has their role been so significant as in the island kingdom of Ceylon. The *Mahāvamso* narrates that when one day, in the first year of his reign, king Iḷanāga (A. D. 95–A. D. 101) had been to the Tissa tank, many of the Laṃbakarṇas, who were an important clan in Laṅkā, deserted him and went back to the capital. When the king saw them not, he was wrath, and as a punishment he ordered that they themselves should make a road to the Mahāthūpa. He further commanded that they should stamp it down firmly, where it ran beside a tank, and set Cāṇḍālas to be their overseers. Full of anger because of this, the Laṃbakarṇas came together, took the king captive, imprisoned him and in his place they themselves administered the government. But king Iḷanāga escaped, raised an army, and gave battle to the Laṃbakarṇas. They were finally beaten. The victorious king ordered that the Laṃbakarṇas were to be yoked two and two behind one another to his triumphal car, and thus did he enter the capital in front of them. At the instance of his mother, king Iḷanāga did not strike off their heads but only had their noses and toes cut off.[95] These Laṃbakarṇas, as they are called in history of Ceylon, gave that island a dynasty about which we shall not say anything here.[96]

The tradition of these Laṃbakarṇas has survived till our own days. Even Mandeville was constrained to include notices of these curious people in his travels. He writes that in the Indian Ocean were " in another isle (be) folk that have great ears and long, that hung down to their knees."[97]

With the testimony of Pliny, the *Mahāvamso*, and

Mandeville before us, it is difficult to discredit the inclusion of the Laṃbakarṇa-deśa as one of the fifty-six conventional divisions mentioned by the Hindu lexicographers.[98] Likewise is it not possible to dismiss as traditional bombast and poetical exaggeration the following notices found in the inscriptions of the Karṇāṭaka trading classes.

It has to be admitted that evidence is not forthcoming to show what part the Laṃbakarṇas played in the history of the mainland before they migrated to Ceylon. But it is permissible to assume that they were of the same stock to which the Karṇaprāvarṇas, the Aṣṭakarṇas, the Oṣṭakarṇas, and the Naikapriṣṭas belonged.[99] Of these the Naikapriṣṭas, *i. e.*, those who had more than one back, have left hardly any trace behind them. Likewise has history nothing to say for the present of the Aṣṭakarṇas or the people who had eight ears.

The traditions of the Oṣṭakarṇas, who had lips extended to their ears, however, remained in the country till the days of Mandeville. This traveller tells us that "in another isle (in the Indian Ocean) be folk of foul fashion and shape that have the lip above the mouth so great, that when they sleep in the sun they cover all the face with that lip."[100]

We have more definite evidence of the Karṇaprāvarṇas or those who wrapped themselves in their ears. These were identical with the Enātoitai described by Megasthenes as a people who had ears hanging down to their feet so that they could sleep upon them.[101]

The Karṇaprāvarṇas were known to India long before the days of Megasthenes. They are mentioned in the *Mahābhārata* on the following occasions:— Innumerable Karṇaprāvarṇas along with the Vaṅgas, the Kaliṅgas, the Māgadhas, and others waited at the gate to receive the audience of Yudhiṣṭira. They were told by the gate-keeper that if they could wait and bring good tribute, they would be admitted. Then the kings of those nations gave each a thousand elephants furnished with tusks like unto the shafts of ploughs, and decked with girdles made of gold and covered with fine blankets, and, therefore, resembling the lotus hue. And they were all darkish as rocks, and always musty. They were procured from the sides of the Kāmyaka lakes and covered with defensive armour.[102] The association of the Karṇaprāvarṇas with the Vaṅgas and the Kaliṅgas suggests that they were reckoned to be a people who hailed from the eastern regions.

But like the other wild tribes, the Karṇaprāvarṇas had also made the southern tracts their home even in the times of the *Mahābhārata* itself. We infer this from the following description of Sahadeva's conquests. After defeating Mainda and Dvividha in the Kiṣkindhyā region, and likewise the king of (the southern) Māhiṣmatī, Sahadeva brought under subjection numberless kings of the Mleccha tribes living on the sea coast, and the Niṣādas and the cannibals, and even the Karṇaprāvarṇas, and those tribes called Kālamukhas, who were a cross between human beings and the Rākṣasas.[103]

The Kālamukhas mentioned in the *Mahābhārata* are also referred to in the *Rāmāyaṇa*.[104] These black faced tribes together with the Lohamukhas or those with the faces of a harsh iron-like colour, were, according to Gerini, the Indo-Chinese Negritos; while the Karṇaprāvarṇas and the Oṣṭakarṇas-the former of whom, according to the same writer, had ear flaps as wide as a sheet, and the latter ears that reached to their lips, - were the tribes of Moñ-Khmer and of hybridized Negrito stock whom the Chinese of the Han period called Tan-erh, or "Drooping ears", and after whom they named the western division of Hainan in B. C. 110. These are the stiff hair tufted Li, the Le, Loi, or the Löi of other parts of Indo-China, "whose ears reach down to their shoulders", inhabiting the hill tracts as well as the sea shore, and Ptolemy's cave dwelling Lestai.[105]

The Karṇaprāvarṇa and the Lambakarṇas are not the only two tribes whom the Greek geographers noticed in India and whom they classified among the Kirātas. There was another tribe which came under their observation, and it was made up of the Ekapādas. These are called the Okupedes, the Okypedes, the Sciapodae, and the Monocoli by the Greek geographers. They were a people who are supposed to have had only one foot; and who were noted for their swiftness of foot.[106] Pliny quoting Ktesias says that the latter also speaks of another race of men, who are known as Monocoli, who have only one leg but who are able to leap with surprising agility. The same people were called Sciapodae, because they were in the habit of lying on their backs, during the time of the extreme heat, and protect themselves from the sun by the shade of their feet. These people, Ktesias says, dwell not very far from the Troglodytae (dwellers in caves).[107]

Once again we may revert to the age of the *Mahābhārata* in order to confirm the statements of the Greek writers and of the composers of *s'āsanas* whom we shall presently cite. Among the numerous princes and chieftains who came to the court of Yudhiṣṭira to pay him homage, were tribes who hailed from different regions. Some possessed two eyes, some three, and some whose eyes were on their foreheads and those also called Ausnikas, and Niṣādas, and Romakas, and some that were cannibals, and many possessing only one leg. These stood at the gate being refused permission to enter. And then they brought as tribute ten thousand asses of diverse hues and black necks and huge bodies and great speed and much docility and celebrated all over the world. These asses, we may add, were all from the coast of Vaṅkhu.[108]

The same epic gives us another name of the Ekapādas while describing the southern conquests of Sahadeva. After conquering the Kālamukhas, the whole of the Cole mountains, Surabhipaṭṭaṇa, the Copper Island, and the mountain called Rāmaka, he subjugated the king Timingala and then conquered a wild tribe known by the name of the Keraka and who were men with only one leg.[109]

The *Mārkaṇḍeya Purāṇa* locates the Ekapādas, whom it wrongly calls Ekapādapas, between the Tāmraliptas and the Vardhamānas.[110] In another connection it mentions them after Annadārakas and before the Khās'as. And the same work places them in the Tortoise's north-east foot.[111]

The *Bṛhatsaṃhitā* confirms the evidence of the earlier writers as regards the existence of the Ekapādas. According to it, they lived in the eastern division.[112]

Mandeville has something to say about them too. In the Indian Ocean, he writes, is an island with folk that have horse's feet. "And they be so strong and mighty, and swift runners; for they take wild beasts while running, and eat them."[113]

The same traveller has an account of another people. These were the inhabitants of an island which he calls Dondun. Here were folk, writes Mandeville, " of great stature. And they be hideous for to look upon. And they have but one eye, and that is in the middle of the front. And they eat nothing but raw flesh and raw fish."[114]

We have just seen how among the people and princes who came to the court of Yudhiṣṭira, there were some who had eyes on their foreheads. The *Mārkaṇḍeya Purāṇa* too mentions the Ekakṣaṇas, or the one-eyed people, after the Kalas and before the Vāji-Kes'as.[115]

Inscriptional evidence ranging from the middle of the eleventh century to the end of the fourteenth century A. D. confirms the existence of such tribes. One of the most enterprising people of India were the Vīra Baṇajas who, as is related in an inscription dated A. D. 1050, travelled through the countries of the Ekapādas, Pārasa, Nepāla, Laṃbakarṇas, S'trīrājya, Golāmukha, and others.[116] Guṇḍa Daṇḍādhipa, the great general of the Vijayanagara king Harihara II, is reputed to have conquered many countries among which were those of the Kākamukhas, Ekapādas, Golāmukhas, and others. The record which gives us these and other details is dated about A. D. 1397.[117]

THE YAKSAS AND THE KINNARAS

In a certain sense more celebrated than any of those mentioned above were two tribes who have appeared conspicuosly in Hindu as well as in Buddhist literature. It would be futile to enter into a detailed description of the activities of these two tribes - the Yakṣas and the Kinnaras - as given in the Buddhist or Hindu accounts, in a short survey of the wild tribes like this. For our purpose we may note the grounds on which their identity with the prominent tribes who form the

the subject of this treatise– the Kirātas and others–may be said to rest. And we may adduce such of the references to the Yakṣas and the Kinnaras which are found in Hindu and Buddhist literature, meagre as they will appear to be, in order to complete the picture of some of the most well known wild tribes in Indian history.

The term Kirāta includes, as we have already seen, the Khambu, Limbu, and Yākhā tribes.[118] Further, it was noted that among the Aryan *janapadas* were included the abodes of the Yakṣas, the Kinnaras, the Pulindas, and the Kirātas in the *Matsya Purāṇa.*[119] Their country, as will be presently narrated, was in the beautiful region of Kāśmir. These considerations are enough to justify our inclusion under the designation of wild tribes the Yakṣas and the Kinnaras who, however much they may have been glorified in literature, seem to have been essentially of the stock to which the Beḍars, the S'abaras, and the Kirātas belonged. We shall give a few examples of the great importance to which the Yakṣas rose in Hindu and Buddhist thought. The Yakṣas have been immortalized in the *Bhagavat Gītā* where the Lord Kṛṣṇa says that of the Rudras, He is S'aṅkara, of the Yakṣas and Rākṣasas, the Lord of Wealth (Kubera), of the Vasus, Pāvaka, and of the mountains, Meru.[120] On the Lord revealing His marvellous forms, hosts of Rudras, Ādityas, Vasus, and Sādhyas, Vis've-Devas, and As'vins, Maruts, Uṣmapas, Gandharvas, Yakṣas, Asuras and Siddhas, as Arjuna exclaimed, were looking at Him, all quite astounded.[121]

To whom the Yakṣas were adorable is told by the Lord in his explanation of the three classes of men and the *s'raddhā* peculiar to each :–The *sāttvic* men worship the Devas, the *rājasic*, the Yakṣas and the Rākṣasa; the others, the *tamasic* men, the Pretas and the hosts of Bhūtas.[122]

These notices of the Yakṣas in the *Bhagavat Gītā* do not by any means exhaust the references to these celebrated beings in Hindu literature. Neither do the following selected from the Buddhist literature. That we may have some idea of the importance of the Yakṣas in Buddhist literature, we may give a few instances of Yakṣas figuring as prominent factors in Buddhist history. The Yakṣas, according to the Buddhists, were demons who are frequently represented as eating human flesh. They were capable of assuming different shapes and of moving in the air.[123]

The *Jātakas* contain allusions to the nature and habits of the Yakṣas. The *Vidhurapaṇḍita Jātaka* describes a Yakkha called Puṇṇaka, who, disguised as a Brāhmaṇ youth, carried off the Great Being. The same Yakkha changed himself into a lion, an elephant, and a *nāga*.[124]

When the Yakkha wishing to slay the Boddhisatta, as narrated in the *Ayakūṭa Jātaka*, stood at the bed's head of the Boddhisatta, the throne of S'akka manifested signs of heat. After considering the matter, the god discovered the cause and grasping the thunderbolt in his hand, came and stood over the Yakkha. The latter did not kill the Boddhisatta for fear of S'akka[125]

In the *Jagadissa Jātaka* we are informed that the eyes of the Yakkhas, like those of other ogres, are red and do not wink. They cast no shadow and are free from all fear.[126]

A male Yakkha falls in love with the beautiful queen Sambulā, wife of the leper king Sotthisena. And the *Sambula Jātaka*, which gives us these details, describes the Yakkha as seizing her by the hand and threatening her with the words–"Unless you obey my words, I will eat you alive."[127] A certain Yakkha is described in the *Dhonasāka Jātaka* as coming from his watch-tower and tearing off the right eye of king Brahmadatta's son.[128] When the Boddhisatta was leading a caravan through a forest, as is narrated in the *Gumbiya Jātaka*, a certain Yakkha named Gumbiya strewed leaves on a spot in the middle of the forest, and dropping some pieces of honey, covered them with deadly poison, and himself wandered all about the road, pretending to tap the trees, as if he were looking for honey. In their ignorance, the men mistook it for honey, ate it and died.[129]

The *Mahāvamso* confirms the evil nature of the Yakṣas as given in the *Jātakā* stories. In the reign of king Sirisaṅgabodhi, a Yakkha named Ratakkhi (red-eye) made red the eyes of the people. If the people did but see one another and did not speak of the redness of the eyes, they died forthwith. And the Yakkha devoured them without fear.[130] This was evidently the worst feature of the Yakṣas. The queen-consort of king Brahmadatta of Benares, as the *Padakusaḷamanava Jātaka* relates, became after her death a female Yakkhā with the face of a horse, because of her sins. She devoured men who frequented the road leading from the eastern to the western border.[131]

The *Mahāvamso* also contains accounts of Yakṣas who could transform themselves into different beings. Vijaya vanquished a Yakkhiṇī who, disguised as a woman hermit, hurled all his seven hundred followers into a chasm.[132] Later on this Yakkhiṇī, being still unable to overcome him, transformed herself into a lovely maiden and became his wife.[133] In the story of the adventures of king Paṇḍukābhya, we have a Yakkhiṇī who transformed herself into a mare with a white body and red feet.[137]

The Yakṣas, therefore, moulded the destiny of Ceylon. The *Mahāvamso* contains further allusions to their chief city and their activities in Ceylon. We are told in that chronicle that as a great sacrifice by Kassapa of Uruvelā (*i. e.*, Buddha Gayā) was near at hand, the Conqueror, in the ninth month of his Buddhahood of the full moon of Phussa, himself set forth for the isle of Laṅkā, to win over that land for the faith. For it was known to the Conqueror as a place where his doctrine should (thereafter) shine in glory; and (he knew that) from Laṅkā, filled as it was with Yakkhas, they must first be driven out. And he also knew that in the midst of Laṅkā, on the fair river bank, in the delightful Mahānāga garden, three *yojanas* wide, the (customary) meeting place for the Yakkhas, there was a great gathering of (all) the Yakkhas dwelling in that island. The Blessed One went there, struck terror in their hearts by rain, storm, darkness, etc., but released them from fear.[135] The Yakkha city in Laṅkā was called Sirīsavatthu.[136]

But, according to Buddhist conceptions, the Yakkhas were not altogether devoid of virtues. Thus in the *Dhammādhamma Putta Cariyama*, we are told that when the Boddhisatta was a great Yakkha named Dhamma with supernatural power, he had compassion on all the world. He was engaged in performing virtuous deeds. Surrounded by his followers, he used to go from place to place. A miserly (mean) Yakkha committing ten evil deeds, also used to go from place to place with his followers. These two were enemies to each other.

Once their cars collided while going in opposite directions. It resulted in a quarrel between the two as regards the right of crossing the road. If Dhamma (only) grew angry with his enemy, or if he had broken his meritorious deeds, he could have turned his enemy with all his followers into particles (of ashes). But in order to protect his *sīla*, he controlled himself and along with his followers allowed his enemy to go along the path. As his rival with his followers was, however, crossing the road, the earth opened wide and swallowed them up.[137]

The allusions to the Yakṣas as given in the *Mahāvamso* would lead one to suppose that they were natives only of the island of Ceylon. But this does not seem to be the case at all. From the *Mahāvamso* itself we learn that they were confined to the Himālayan regions as well. The *Rājataraṅgiṇī* confirms this, while the works of Kālidāsa and Abhinava Pampā bring them to the Vindhyan tracts in the sixth and tenth centuries of the Christian era.

A definite reference to the Himālayan habitat of the Yakṣas is found in the *Ayakūṭa Jātaka* which narrates that when the Boddhisatta seeing that men were addicted to animal sacrifices, proclaimed by beat of drum that no living creature was to be put to death, the Yakkhas living in the Himālayas became angry at the Boddhisatta for cheating them of their offering. They then called together an assembly of their tribes and sent forth a certain savage Yakkha to slay the Boddhisatta. This Yakkha took a huge blazing mass of iron as big as the dome of a house, and wishing to strike a deadly blow immediately after the mid-watch, came and stood at the bed's head of the Boddhisatta. But, as narrated above, S'akka frightened him and drove him away.[138]

The *Rājataraṅgiṇī* of Kalhaṇa also locates the Yakṣas on the Himālayas, especially in Kās'mir. In the legend of king Dāmodara Suda II it is said that he endeavoured to get long stone-lined dykes built in his country by the Yakṣas, in order to guard against inundations.[139]

Referring to the rise of Hinduism in Kās'mir, Kalhaṇa informs us that as the first Candradeva had stopped the plague of the Yakṣas, so the second (of that name) brought to an end in that land the intolerable plague of the Bhikṣus.[140]

Mihirakula's name is also associated with the Yakṣas in the following context in the same work. When he was diverting the water of the river called Candrakulyā, a rock in its middle, which could not be moved, impeded the work. Then Mihirakula performed a penance and was told in a dream by the gods that a powerful Yakṣa, who observed the vow of chastity, lived in that rock; and that it could be removed only when touched by a chaste woman. It is interesting to observe that a potter's wife named Candrāvatī alone could remove it.[141]

Of Pravarasena II it is said in the same historical narrative that he discovered the measuring line which the Vetāla (Rākṣasa) had laid down at the village S'ārīṭaka, where the goddess S'ārikā and the Yakṣa demon Aṭṭa resided.[142]

The fact of the Yakṣas having made Kās'mir their home in the north and Ceylon in the south being thus confirmed by Hindu and Buddhist sources, it remains to be seen whether there is any evidence of their having occupied the Vindhya regions as well. In the celebrated lyric piece *Meghadūta*, the Yaksa who is condemned by his master Kubera, takes up his abode on Rāmagiri in the Vindhya mountains.[143] In the *Meghadūta* we have another example of a Yakṣa being raised to the highest pinnacle of poetical glory in Hindu literature.

On many occasions the Yakṣas appear on the scene in the *Das'ākumāracarita*. The queen Vasumatī is presented with an infant boy by a Yakṣa girl named Tārāvali. With the consent of the king of the Yakṣas, she had given the boy to the queen, so that he might serve her son Rājavāhana. Who and where this king of the Yakṣas was, we cannot make out. But the incident seems to have taken place in the forests of the Vindhyas.[144] In other passages, Daṇḍin portrays the Yakṣas as evil spirits.[145]

Abhinava Pampā introduces a Yakṣa king in the forest of the Vindhyas.[146]

The Yakṣas have often been ushered in history and literature along with another people–the Kinnaras. Like the Yakṣas they too have been represented in Hindu mythology as attendants on Kubera. They are not unknown to Buddhist literature. The Great Being gathered fruit with a band of Kinnaras, on the mountains, and returned at evening time home, as is narrated in the *Sāma Jātaka*.[147]

The characteristic feature of the Kinnaras as given in Hindu literature, *viz.*, that of being celestial musicians, is also mentioned in the *Jātakas*. In the *Takkariya Jātaka* it is related that a hunter while up in the regions of the Himālayas, by some means or other captured a brace of supernatural beings, a nymph and her husband, and then took them as a present to the king. It was then that the hunter related that the captured creatures could sing with a honey voice and dance delightfully, and that no man could sing or dance so beautifully as they could.[148] A Barhut relief strikingly illustrates this scene from the *Takkariya Jātaka*, and incidentally justifies our inclusion of the Kinnaras among the Kirātas, some tribes akin to whom, under the appellation of Parṇa-S'abaras, wore leaves. This relief in the Barhut Stūpa depicts the Kinnara couple mentioned above, in front of the king, up to their knees and wearing leaves of trees round the body.[149]

The Kinnaras were sweet creatures. The *Aṭṭasadda Jātaka* speaks of a pair of Kinnaras who plucked and decked themselves with many flowers of choice hue and scent, and never noticed that the sun was setting and that darkness was falling as they were descending a hill.[150]

The *Jātakas* also represent the Kinnaras as fairies and elves. One such Kinnara was Rahavatī who dwelt in a tree. She was married to a Brāhmaṇa hermit named Vaccha, as is told in the *Mahā Ummagga Jātaka.*[151]

The *Caṅda Kinnara Jātaka* contains picturesque details regarding the location of the Kinnaras and their sportive habits. Once while king Brahmadatta was ruling at Benares, the Boddhisatta was born as a Kinnara on the Himālayas. His wife was named Caṅdā. These two Kinnaras dwelt on a mountain top called Caṅdapabbata. Tho king Brahmadatta entrusting the care of his government over to the charge of his ministers, wearing two yellow robes, and taking with him five weapons, left his capital and entered the regions of the Himālayas. There he lived on the flesh of the deer. Following the course of a rivulet, he ascended the Caṅdapabbata.

Now, the Kinnaras who dwelt on this mountain were accustomed to descend to the lower plains only in summer and not in the rainy season. (At such a time) Caṅda Kinnara and his wife Caṅdā, anointing themselves with sandal wood paste, eating the pollen of flowers, attiring themselves in apparel made of flowers, swinging on creeper singing sweetly, came to that same rivulet which king Brahmadatta had reached. There they sported in water scattering flowers around. Again wearing flower gauze, they prepared a couch of flowers on the silvery sands of the river. Then taking a bamboo flute, they took their seat on the flowery couch. Caṅda Kinnara began to play on the flute and sang sweetly (too). At this Candā manipulating her hands, danced at a little distance from him. It was at this juncture that king Brahmadatta, falling in love with Caṅdā, determined to kill her husband, in order to win her for himself. In the advice which S'akka, who had come to the scene having been invoked by Caṅdā, gave her, when she lay pierced by a shaft from the quiver of the king, almost on the point of dying, *viz.*, that they–the Kinnaras-should never leave their mountain homes[152] and tread the path of men–,we have an explanation of the fact of the Kinnaras having been confined only to the poetic regions of the Himālayas and of their absence in general in the world of men.

It is very interesting to mention here the happy discovery by Professor Jitendra Nath Banerjee of a Gāndhāra relief in the Indian Museum at Calcutta, representing a version of the same *Caṅda Kinnara Jātaka* and showing the Kinnara couple as two ordinary human beings clothed in heavy drapery peculiar to the locality (*viz.*, the Swat Valley in the North Western

Frontier from which place this fragmentary relief hails).[153]

That the Hindu authors also associated the Himālayan regions with the Kinnaras is proved by the statements in the *Meghadūta* and the *Kādambari*. In the former Kālidāsa writes thus while describing the snow clad Himālayas which the Cloud had to visit:—There the bamboos, as they are filled with the wind, produce pleasing sounds while the victory over Tripura is sung in chorus by the wives of the Kinnaras: if your thunder, then, resounding in the caves, will be as deep as the sound of the tabor, the apparatus of S'iva's concert there will surely be complete.[154] Then, again, the Kinnaras are introduced in the city of Kubera, Alakā, thus:—Where lovers, having inexhaustible treasure in their houses and accompanied by celestial damsels, the best courtezans, enjoy every day holding conversations in the outer garden called Vaibharāja, in company with the Kinnaras having a melodious voice and singing loudly the glory of Kubera.[155]

We have already remarked how Kālidāsa, while dealing with the expeditions of Raghu and the northern habitat of the Kinnaras, describes the Kinnaras living on the Himālayas. Together with the Utsavasaṅketas they were conquered by Raghu.

Bāṇa's evidence seems to confirm that of his predecessors in regard to the northern home of the Kinnaras. Mahāsveta tells Caṅdrāpīḍa that Hemakūṭa was pleasant, the royal city of Citraratha marvellous, the Kinnara country curious, the Gandharva world beautiful, and Kādambarī noble and generous of heart.[156]

NOTES

CHAPTER I

POLICY OF THE HINDU RULERS TOWARDS THE WILD TRIBES

1. How their presence in the country has been ignored and the havoc they caused underestimated, may be seen from the statements of modern writers on Indian history. Dr. Vincent Smith wrote thus in his *Early History of India* :—" In those days vast territories were still covered by forest, the home of countless wild beasts and scanty tribes of savage men; while regions of great extent in Northern India had been occupied for untold centuries by more or less civilized communities of the highest races who, from time to time, during the unrecorded past, had pierced the mountain barriers of the north-western frontier." *Early History*, p. 28. Oxford, 1914.

2. McCrindle, *India as described by Ktesias*, pp. 23-24. Calcutta, 1882.

3. *Ibid*, p. 86.

4. *Arthas'āstra*, Bk. II, Ch. I., p. 51, Shama Sastry, Mysore, 1923.

5. *Ibid*, Bk. III. Ch. XVI. pp. 366-7.

6 & 7. *Ibid*, Bk. VIII. Ch. IV. p. 389.

8. *Ibid*, Bk. IX. Ch. III. p. 403.

9. *Ibid*, Bk. X. Ch. II. p. 423.

10. *Ibid*, Bk. IX. Ch. I. p. 397.

11. *Ibid*, Ch. II. p. 400.

12. *Ibid*, Bk. VII. Ch. VIII. p. 343. The five kinds of armies mentioned by Kauṭalya gave place to six in the times of Kālidāsa. *Raghuvaṁs'a*, IV, 26. Mallinātha explains the six kinds of armies thus :— *maulāḥ* or those who are born and here-

18

ditary soldiers; *bhṛtyāḥ* or those who are paid soldiers; *suhṛdāḥ* or those who are allies; *s'reṇayaḥ* or mercenary soldiers; *diviṣadaḥ* or those who are won over from the enemy's camp (or those who are ill-disposed towards him against whom a campaign is conducted;) and finally, *āṭavikāḥ* or those who comprise wild tribes.

13. *Arthas'āstra*, Bk. IX. Ch. II. p. 400.
14. *Ibid*, p. 401.
15. *Ibid*, Ch. III. p. 403.
16. *Ibid*, Bk. VII. Ch. VIII. p. 343.
17. *S'ukranīti*, I. ll. 506–12, p. 34. (Sarkar, Allahabad, 1913).
18. *Ibid*, IV. Sec. vii. 11. 27–28, p. 217. Bṛhaspati has some remarks to make on wild tribes attached to armies. *Bṛhaspati*, p. 241 (*SBE* Vol. XXXII.). For some notes on wild tribes, read *The Indian Antiquary*, VI. pp. 133–35.
19. *S'ukranīti*, IV. Sec. v. ll. 44–45, p. 185.
20. Hultzsch, *Corpus Inscriptionum Indicarum (Edicts of As'oka)* I. p. 95.
21. *Ibid*, p. 62.
22. *Ibid*, pp. 99–100.
23. *Ibid*, p. 127.
24 & 25. *Ibid*, pp. 69, 70.
26. *Ibid*, p. 52.
27. *Ibid*, pp. 105–106.
28. *Āmuktamālyada*, IV. 206; *Journal of Indian History*, IV. p. 65.
29. *Āmuktamālyada*, IV. 224; *JIH*, IV. p. 67.
30 *Āmuktamālyada*, IV. 256; *JIH*, IV. p. 72.
31. *Āmuktamālyada*, IV. 221; *JIH*, IV. p. 66.
32. *Āmuktamālyada*, IV 225; *JIH*, IV. p. 67.
33. *Āmuktamālyada*, IV. 222–223, 257; *JIH*, IV. pp. 67–72.

CHAPTER II

THE KIRĀTAS

1. *Manu*, X. 43–44, See also *ibid* pp. 412–13 (SBE. Vol. XXV), Calcutta, 1904.
2. Pargiter, *Mārkaṇḍeya Purāṇa*, pp. 322, *n*. 333, Calcutta 1904.
3. *Mahābhārata*, Anus'āsana Parva, XXXV, p. 226; As'-medha Parva, XXIV, p. 74 ; Sabhā Parva, XIV, LII, pp. 44, 145. (Roy) Cf. *Bhagavat Gītā*, pp. 294–5. (SBE. Vol. VIII).
4. McCrindle, *India as described by Megasthenes and Arrian*, pp. 75, n., 132, n. Calcutta, 1877.
5. McCrindle, *Ancient India as described by Ptolemy*, pp. 191–92, Calcutta. 1885.
6. Gerini, *Researches into Ptolemp's Geography of Eastern Asia*, p. 28 London, 1909.
7. *Ibid*, pp. 51–52. See also Dey, *Geographical Dicty. of Ancient and Mediaeval India*, p. 100, 2nd ed. London, 1927.
8. *Sabhā Parva*, XXX, p. 86.
9. *Udyoga Parva*, XIX. p. 43.
10. *Sabhā Parva*, XXVI. p. 79.
11. *Vana Parva*, LI. p. 155.
12. *Sabhā Parva*, IV. p. 9.

13 & 14. *Bhīs'ma Parva*, IX. pp. 32-33.

15 & 16. *Viṣṇu Purāṇa*. pp. 175, 190. (Wilson, London, 1840) Cf. *Garuḍa Purāṇa* Ch. 55, V. 5, p. 139, where it is stated that the Kirātas live in the east, the Yavanas in the west, the Āndhras in the south, and the Turuṣkas in the north.

17. *Mārkaṇḍeya Purāṇa*, p. 284.
18. *Agni Purāṇa*. I. CXVIII. p. 473 (Dutt, Calcutta, 1903–4. 2 Vols.).
19. *Mārkaṇḍeya Purāṇa*, p. 322.
20. *Ibid*, pp. 345, 347.
21. *Ibid*, p. 369.
22. *Ibid*, p. 379.
23. *Ibid*, p. 383.
24. *Ibid*, p. 369, n.
25. *Matsya Purāṇa*, I. CXIV, p. 307. (Taluqdar, Sacred Books of the Hindus Series).
26. *Ibid*, p. 308.
27. *Ibid*, CXXI, p. 327.
28. *Ibid*, CXIV, p. 310.
29. *Bṛhatsaṁhitā*, XIV, 18, 29–30, pp. 90, 92. (Kern., Calcutta, 1895). The *Bṛhatsaṁhitā* also speaks of a Kirāta king. *Ibid*, IX. 17 ; XI. 54. See also *Bhāgavata Purāṇa*, II, 4. 18 ; IX, 20, 30.
30. *Raghuvaṁs'a*, IV. 77-78.
31. *Kādambarī*, Purv. p. 270. Kane, Bombay, 1914. See also, p. 90 Ridding (Miss), London, 1896.
32. *As'vamedha Parva*, LXXXIII, p. 209.
33. *Sabhā Parva*, XXXII, p. 94.
34. *Ibid*, XXXI. p. 87.
35. Abhinava Pampā, *Pampā Bhārata* VII. p. 157. Rice Bangalore, 1898. For his date, *ibid*, Intr. p. 1.
36. Pampā, *Rāmāyaṇa*, VII. vv. 109–115, pp. 193-5. Rice, Bangalore, 1892.
37. Nijaguṇayogi, *Vivekacintāmaṇi*, pp. 423-4. Bangalore, 1893.
38. Risley, *Castes and tribes of Bengal*, I. p. 490.
39. Banerjee, *Journal of the Asiatic Society of Bengal* for 1873, No. 187 ; IA, III. pp. 178–9.

40. Bird, *The Political and Statistical History of Gujarat*, Intr. p. 10 ; London, MDCCCXXXV.

41. Rose, *A Glossary of the Tribes and Castes of the Panjab and North-West Frontier Provinces, etc.* I., pp. 634–5. Lahore, 1919.

42. *Journal of the Royal Asiatic Society* for 1925, p. 236 and *ibid*, n. (1). Grierson maintains that the word *citada* is the same as Kirāta. *Ibid*, pp. 234–5.

43. *Rāmāyaṇa*, Kiṣk. Kaṇḍa, XL. 30. Gorresio, Parigi. M. DCCCXLIII. Gerini locates them on the Indo--Chinese seaboard. *Ptolemy*, p. 256, n.

44. *Sabhā Parva*, LVII. p. 144.

45. *Droṇa Parva*, CXII. pp. 321–2.

46. McCrindle, *India as described by Megasthenes and Arrian*, pp. 173–4.

47. *Das'akumāracarita*, Purv. Ucch. II.p. 24. Bombay, 1925. See also S'ri Harṣa Deva, *Ratnāvali*, II. 29, p. 21, Bombay, 1882.

48. *Das'akumāracarita*, Purv. Ucch. III. p. :104. The author calls the Kirāta also Bhilla and Lubdhaka. *Ibid*, pp. 103-4.

49. *Ibid*, Ucch. VIII. p. 203.

50. Narasimācārya *Kavicarite*, II. p. 219, Bangalore, 1924

51. *Mārkaṇḍeya Purāṇa*, Ch. LXXXII. vv. 10–18.

52. *Ibid*, pp. 473-74.

53. Hiranandu Sastri, *Memoirs of the Archaeological Survey of India*, No. 20, p. 12.

54. *Mārkaṇḍeya Purāṇa*, Ch. II. v. 107 Ck. *Das'akumāracarita*, Ucch. VIII. p. 204, where the goddess Vindhyāvāsinī is pictured as a prophet and a saviouress.

55. Hirananda Sastri, *ibid*, p. 16.

56. *Ibid*, p, 12.

57. Foucher, *Iconographie buddhique*, p. 78.

58. Das, *JASB*, II. p. 116.

59. *Epigraphia Indica*, XI. p. 302. See also Pargiter, *Mark. Purāṇa*, Intr. pp. xiii-xiv, where *Devī Māhātmya* is said to be not later than the ninth century A. D. There is every reason to suggest that this Vindhyan deity had travelled as far as the Sahyas or the northern part of the Western Ghats. See *Mṛcchakaṭika*, X. p. 279. I am indebted to my colleague Professor K. N. Watwe for this reference. B. A. S.

60. *Das akumāracarita*, Purv. Ucch. I. pp. 14-15, Ucch. VI. p. 149. See also *ibid*, Ucch. VIII. p. 206 where Vindhyāvāsinī is called Durgā.

61. *Harivaṁs'a*, Ch. LVIII. vv. 6–8. Calcutta, 1897.

62. *Devi Māhātmya* as given in the *Mārk. Purāṇa* pp. 474-5.

63. *Kādambarī*, pp. 331 seq. (Kale, 1914. 3rd. ed.); pp. 94-98 (Kane, 2nd ed. 1914.).

64. *Epigraphia Carnatica*, VII. Sk. 137, p. 104; Rice, *Mysore and Coorg from the Inscriptions*, pp. 72–3.

65. *EC.* XII. Tp. 61, p. 55.

66. *128 of the Madras Epigraphical Report for the year* 1901 ; *South Indian Inscriptions*, VII. No. 328, p.168.

67. *EC.* VIII. Tl. 13, p. 165.

68. Cf. *JASB* for 1873, *op. cit.*

69. *Bhīs'ma Parva*, L. p. 186.

70. *Karṇa Parva* LXXIII. p. 271.

71. *Droṇa Parva*, CXIX. p. 349.

72. & 73. *Smith, EHI.*, pp. 93, 107.

74 & 75. Bostock-Riley, *The Natural History of Pliny*, II. pp. 59, and *ibid*, n, (39), 60. London, MDCCCLV.

76. *Ptolemy*, Bk. VI. cap. 12, sec. 4; Gerini, *Ptolemy*, p. 830, n. (1).

77. *Muarārākṣasa*, II. See also *ibid* Act. III where on the occasion of the feigned quarrel, Cānakya tells Candragupta about the officers who, dissatisfied with Candragupta's government, had

sought service under Malayaketu. The latter was preparing to attack Candragupta with a large army of Mlecchas.

78. Bühler, *JRAS* for 1898. p. 386; Smith, *EHI*. pp. 283-4.

79. Fleet, *Cor. Inscr. Ind.*, III. p, 13.

80. Smith, *ibid.*

81. A. V. Venkatrama Iyer, *JIH*, I p. 86.

82. Fleet, *ibid*, pp. 114, 116.

83. *Bṛhatsamhitā*, XIV. 29-30

84. *EC*. III. Md. 113, p. 51.

85. *EC*. II. p. 119 (1st ed.)

86. *EC*. XII. Si. 28, p. 92; Rice, *Mys. A Gazetteer*, I. p. 307 (rev. ed.)

87. *EC*. III. TN. 44, p. 76.

88. *EC*. IV. Ch. 83, p. 10.

89. *EC*. VII. Sh. 2. p. 3.

90. *Mysore Inscriptions*, p. 310; Rice, *Mysore and Coorg*., pp. 129-130

CHAPTER III

THE S'ABARAS

1. *Amarakos'a*, II, 20-21.

2. *Arthas'āstra*, p. 46. (text). Mysore, 1909. Dr. Shama Sastry translates the word S'abara into archer, and Pulinda, hunter. Trans. p. 49.

3 *Das'akumāracarita*, Pur. pp. 14-15. *op. cit.*

4. *Aitareya Brāhmaṇa*, VII. 18. Cf. *S'ankhāyana Sūtra*, XV. 16.

5. *Ādi Parva*, CLXXVII. p. 504. Cunningham has some interesting observations to make on the name S'abara.

He traces the origin of the word to the Scythian *sagari* meaning an axe. ASR., XVII. p. 113.

6. McCrindle, *India as described by Megasthenes*, p. 149. In a note on the same page, McCrindle identifies the S'abaras with the Sauviras.
7. Pliny, *Nat. Hist.* VI. 22, 6 ; McCrindle, *IA.* VI. p. 127
8. McCrindle, *Ptolemy*, p. 172.
9. *Rāmāyaṇa*, Ādi kāṇḍa, I. p. 59 ; Araṇya kāṇḍa, LXXVII. 6–32.
10. *Ibid*, Araṇya kāṇḍa, LXXI, 23, 26.
11. *Bṛhatsaṃhitā*, XIV, 9–10, p. 89.
12. *Ibid*, XVI. I, P. 99.
13. *Ibid*, p. 29.
14. *IA*. XXII. p. 188.
15. Gerini, *Ptolemy*, pp, 749, 808. Cunningham had of course pointed this out long ago, as will be seen presently.

16. & 17. *Mārkaṇḍeya Purāṇa*, pp. 335, 361.

18. *Matsya Purāṇa*, I. Ch. CXIV. p. 309. In the *Bhāgavata Purāṇa* the S'abaras are mentioned as a low caste. II. 7, 46 (Bombay Skt. Series).

19. Cunningham, *Ancient Geography of India*, pp. 508–9 (1st ed). Mr. Charles Oldham conjectures that in the first centuries of the Christian era, they occupied the inland hill and jungle country to the south and south-east of the modern Ranchi district watered by the Brāhmaṇī and its tributaries, and by the Ib and the other tributaries of the Mahānadī. *Journal of the Bihar and Orissa Research Society*, XIII. P. 198. Cunningham had already found them extending from the Mahānadī down to the sea-coast of Ganjam. See below *ASR*, XXI. pp. 94-5.

20 & 21. Cunningham *ASR*, XXI. pp. 94–5.

22. McCrindle, *Ptolemy*, pp. 173 ; Oldham, *ibid*.

23. McCrindle, *ibid*.

24. Risley, *Castes and Tribes of Bengal,* II. pp. 241–246; *The Madras Census Report for 1891,* p. 254; Pargiter *Mārkaṇḍeya Purāṇa,* p. 335. n.; Gerini, *Ptolemy,* p. 73.

25. Cunningham, *ASR.* XXI. p. 93. On Sagar, a *jāgīr* in the Shāhpur town of the Gulburga district, read *Epigraphia Indica,* XII. pp. 272-3.

26. Pargiter, *Mārkaṇḍeya Purāṇa,* p. 361, n. The Gonds too perhaps belonged to the same tribe. Oppert, *Original Inhabitants of the Bhāratvarṣa* Intr. p. 110, and *ibid,* n. (70). Westminister, 1893.

27. *Journal of the Royal Anthropological Institute* for 1875, IV. p. 376. n.; Gerini, *Ptolemy,* p. 808.

28. Rice, *Mysore-A Gazetteer,* pp. 209-210.

29. *Kādambari, Purv.* p. 12. (Kane, Bombay. 1920).

30. *Ibid. Purv.* pp. 27-8 (Ridding).

31. *Mahābhārata, Ādi Parva,* CXXXII.

32 & 33. *Kādambari* pp. 28-30 (Ridding).

34. *Kavicarite,* II. p. 342

35. Taylor, *A Catalogue Raisonee of Oriental Manuscripts,* III, p. 472. Madras, 1857-1862.

36. *Mudrārākṣasa,* V. v. 11. p. 75 (text). In the same drama we are told that five Mleccha kings–Citravāhana of Kulūta, Simhanāda of Malayades'a, Pus'karākṣa of Kās'mira, Sindhus'ena of Sindhudes'a, Meghakoṣa, the lord of the Pārasikas–followed the lead of Rākṣasa. Act I. v. 19. (text). This entire force of the Mlecchas was captured by Cāṇakya, and, later on, put to death. Act V. pp. 78, 82 (text).

37. Geiger-Bode, *Mahavamso,* p. 27. Some maintain that Candragupta was not low-born. *IHQ.,* VIII, p. 466 seq.

38. *Mudrārākṣasa,* Acts I & III ; *ibid,* pp. 4. 38 (trans.).

39. *The Upaniṣads,* v. 13. pp. 218-9 (SBE. XV).

40. *The Sacred Laws of the Aryas*, p. II. p. 243 (*SBE*. XIV.) Cf. The *Gṛhya Sūtras*, p. 87 (*SBE*. XXX).

41. *Manu*, v. 16. p. 255 (SBE. XXV.).

42. *Viṣṇu Purāṇa*, Bk. III. Ch. 10 v. 9 See also *ibid*, Bk. IV. Ch. XXIV. p. 479 (Or. Trans. Fund).

43. *Anuśāsana Parva*, XLVIII. p. 273.

44. *Manu*, X. 34. The *Bhāgavata Purāṇa* calls the Dāsas fishermen. *Bhāgavata Purāṇa*, IX. 22, 20. On the Dāsas, read, H. G. Bengeri, *Annals of the Bhandarkar Oriental Research Institute* for 1927 (Vol. VIII). pp. 295-304.

45. Fleet, *Cor. Inscr. Ind.* III. pp. 16. 28, 44 & 51.

46. *Manu*, X. 22-37. On their origin, read, Fleet, *ibid*, Intr. pp. 185. In Buddhist literature they are represented as a ruling race. Cowell, *Jātakas*, III. p. 1. On their Persian affinities, read *IA*, XXXVII, p. 78, seq. ; on their Tibetan affinities, read *IA*. XXXII. pp. 233-6. Read also Mr. S. Chakravarty's pertinent remarks on their non-Kṣatriya origin, *IHQ*. IX. pp. 439-447.

47. Baudhāyana, *Dharmasūtra*, I. 1, 32 ; Jayaswal, *ABORI*, p. 53. Read also Jayaswal's *History of India*, p. 115.

48. On the expression *svayam magadha kulam* applied to Candragupta, read *Kaumudīmahotsava*, pp. 10, 30 edited by M. R. Kavi and S. K. R. Sastri, Madras, 1929 ; Jayaswal *ABORI*, XII. *ibid*.

49. Fleet, *ibid*, III. p. 293. Read also Muzumdar, *EI*. XI, pp. 103-4.

50. *IA*. VIII. pp. 278–9, 283, seq ; XXII. p. 188 ; *Manual of the Salem Dt.* II. pp. 360, 364 ; *JRAS* (NS) XVII, p. 203 ; Fleet, *ibid*, p. 293.

51. Fleet, *ibid ; Bombay Gazetteer*, I. P. I. pp. 326–27. On Heras's suppositions concerning Udayacandra and Nandivarma, read his *Studies in Pallava History*, pp. 58–59. Madras, 1933.

52. Mahm. Harprasad Sastri, *JASB* for 1902, pp. 2-7; N. N. Vasu, *Modern Buddhim and its Followers in Orissa* Intr. p. 15; Smith, *EHI*. pp. 400, 403, n. (1); R. G. Basak, *EI*. XII. p. 38.

53. Wilson, *Mackenzie Collection*, I. pp. cxx, cxxiv; Rice, *Mysore Inscrp. Intr*. pp. lii-liv.

54. Thurston, *Castes and Tribes of Southern India*, II. pp. 328 seq.; Taylor *Cat. Raisonee*., III. p. 466; Sewell, *Lists of Antiquarian Remains in the Madras Presidency*. I. P. 172. We do not know in what manner they were connected with the Yerkalas, another jungle tribe mentioned in *IA*. IX. p. 210.

55. *EC*. II. Intr. p. 18, n. (7); *EC*. VI. Kd. 147. p. 28. Rice identified Mārasiṅgha with one of the chieftains of the west of the Chitaldroog district. If so, he must himself, as we shall, narrate in a subsequent chapter, have been a Bedar.

56. *Paṁpā Rāmāyaṇa*, IV. vv. 37-8, pp. 82-80.

57. Aiyangar, *The Sources of Vijayanagara History*, pp. 91 98. Madras, 1919. Cf Somanatha, Vyāsayogicaritaṁ, Intr. p. cx. (Ed. Venkoba Rao, Bangalore).

57 (a) Rice, *Mysore and Coorg*, Map.

57 (b) *S'ivattatvaratnākara*, *The Sources*, p. 199.

58. Liṅgaṇṇa, *Keladi Nṛipa Vijaya*, India Office Ms. Copy, pp. 13-4. Dr. R. Shama Sastry's edition of the same work is unfortunately inaccessible to me just as I am writing this book. B. A. S.

59. *Anus'āsana Parva*, XIV. p. 62.

60. & 61. *Paṁpā Rāmāyaṇa*, VIII. v. 14, pp. 269, 121.

62. *Ibid*, IV. v. 16, p. 98.

63. *EC*. II. pp. 19, 120. (1st ed.) See above note 55.

64. *Mysore Archaeological Report for 1913-4*, p. 6.

65. *Jaina Sūtras*, Bk. II. pp. 366-7. (*SBE*. Vol XLV.)

CHAPTER IV

THE BEDARS

I. *JRAS* for 1929, pp. 363-4. Enthoven writes Berads which is evidently an error for Beḍars. B.A.S.

2. Rose, *Castes And Tribes of the Panjab,* I, p. 345.

3. Taylor, *Catalogue Raisonnee,* III. pp. 398, 409; Wilson *Glossary of Indian Terms,* p. 70. This error may be traced to Buchanan, *A Journey from Madras, etc.* I. pp. 358-60. (London, 1807).

4. Taylor, *ibid* pp. 430-1.

5. *Ibid,* p. 398.

6. Sewell, *Lists of Antiquarian Remains.* I p. 148.

7. Crole *Chingleput District Manual,* p. 438 ; Sewell, *ibid,* p. 165.

8. Taylor, *ibid,* pp. 430-1, op. cit.

9. Read Saletore, *Social and Political life in the Vijayanagara Empire,* II. pp. 38-49.

10. Sewell, *ibid,* I. pp. 155, 157, 162, 16), and 191; Crole, *ibid,* pp. 88, 178, 229.

11 & 12. Sewell, *ibid,* pp. 149, 177.

13 & 14. Taylor, *ibid,* pp. 397, 695.

15. On the Kaḷḷars, read Taylor, *Ibid,* pp. 385-6. Relevant portions of Thurston's *Castes and Tribes in Southern India* may also be read with profit. See also *Local Records,* LIII. p. 209.

16-18. Taylor, *ibid,* pp. 464-5, 471.

19. *Ibid,* p. 229.

20. Cunningham, *Ancient Geography of India,* pp. 508-9; *IA.* VI. p. 127. *n.*

21 & 22 *Sabhā Parva,* XXX. pp. 85-6.

23. *Bhīs'ma Parva,* IX. p. 32.

24. Geiger-Bode, *Mahāvamso*, p. 14, and *ibid*, *n*. 2. For further notices of the Mallas, read Pargiter, *Mārkaṇḍeya Purāṇa* pp. 330, and *ibid*, *n*.; Risley, *Castes and Tribes of Bengal*, II. pp. 51, 66; Oppert, *Madras Journal of Literature and Science for 1886*, p. 46 seq. Dr. B. C. Law, *Kṣatriya Clans in Buddhist India*, pp. 162-180. (Calcutta-Simla, 1922). On the defeat of *asura* Malla-from whom is derived the word Mallari, Malahāri (Mailār?)-read, *Bombay Gazetteer*, II. p. 243.

25. *Mālavikāgnimitra*, v. 10, p. 147. (Bombay, 1889.)

26. *Kavicharite*, II. p. 426. (rev. ed. 1924).

27. *Ibid*, p. 199. (1st ed.) See also *ibid*, pp. 247-48, 342. Siddhalinga-yogi calls them in circa 1600 S'abaras. *Ibid*, pp. 323-4.

28. *Mysore Archaeological Report* for 1928, p. 91.

29. *Ibid*, for 1923, p. 83.

30. *EC*. VIII. Sb. 240, p. 37.

31 & 32. *Ibid*, Sb. 202, Sb. 203, p. 32.

33. *EC*. IV. Ng. 23, p.117.

34. Fleet, *Dyn. Kan. Dist.* p. 43. Rice *Mysore and Coorg.*, p. 73.

35. *EC*. VIII. Sb. 184, pp. 29-30.

36 & 37. *Ibid*, Sa. 108 and Sa. 109 (bis), pp. 113-4.

38. Fleet, *ibid*, p. 45.

39. *EC*. VII Sk. 83, pp. 57-8.

40. There is a Barmma Deva in the line of the Kadambas. He was the father of Boppa Deva. Rice, *Mys. and Coorg.* p, 28.

41. *Mysore Archl, Report for 1927*, p. 122.

42 Fleet, *ibid*, p. 49; Rice, *ibid*, p. 73.

43. *EC*. VII. Sk. 205, pp. 128, text, p. 293.

44. Rice, *Mysore Inscriptions*, pp. 173-4.

45. *EC*. VII. Sk. 115. p. 85.

46. *Ibid*, III, 65, p. 172.

47 & 48. *EC*. VIII. Sb. 7, & Sb. 12, pp. 2, 3.

49. *Ibid*, Sb. 175 & 176, p. 25. We do not know whether this Madasale Kāḷarasa was the same Kāḷarasa mentioned in A. D. 1115.

50. *EC*. VII. Sk. 78, p. 56.

51. *EC*. VIII. Sb. 6, p. 2.

52. *EC*. VII. Sk. 75, p. 56.

53. *EC*. VIII. Sb. 249, p 39.

54. *Das'akumāracarita*, Ucch. III. p 104.

55. *JASB*, XL., 347-388; Read also Oppert, *Madras Journal of Literature and Science for 1866*, p. 112, ns. 71 & 72; *IA*. *IV*. pp. 336-8.

56. They were noticed in the south along with the *Mīnavars* (*Mīnas*) by Ptolemy in A. D. 140. See Smith, *EHI*, p. 439.

57. Rice says they were Ceras. *EC*. IX. Intr. pp. 16, 18. Admitting that the Ceras had a bow on their standard, we cannot understand how the statements referring to their complete destruction and to their having been driven to the jungles can be justified if they had been only a people who belonged to the ancient Cera nation.

58. *EC*. IX. Dv. 75, pp. 83–4.

59. *EC*. X. Sd. 66, p. 187.

60. *Ibid*, Kl. 149 (a), p. 52.

61. *EC*. III. Nj. 29, p. 98, TN. 7, p. 70, TN. 71. p. 82.

62. *EC* IX. Nl. 3, p. 30, Kn. 12, p. 122.

63. Rice, *Mysore Gazetteer*, I. p. 311.

64 & 65. Forbes, *Rās Mālā*, pp. 40–41, 43. (1878).

66 & 67. Bird, *History of Gujarat*, pp. 139-40. Forbes says that the date of the foundation of Paṭaṇ was A. D. 746. *Rās Mālā*, pp 28–30.

68. Sewell, *A Forgotten Empire–Vijayanagar*, p. 299, n.(1).

69. Saletore, *Social and Political Life*., I. pp. 83–89.

70. Forbes, *ibid*, p. 136.

71. Tod, *Annals of Rajasthan*, I. Ch. II. pp. 121, 238 seq.; *IA*. XV. p. 275, n.; Fleet, *Cor. Insrcpt. Ind.* III. p. 186, n. (1).

72. Read, *IA*. IV. pp. 336-8 for a fuller account.

73 & 74. Rice, *Mysore and Coorg*. pp. 85-6. In *My Insc.* p. XLV Rice conjectures circa A. D. 894 to be the date of the capture of Talakād by the Coḷas.

75. Rice, *Coorg Inscriptions*, p. 5. (1886).

76. *Ibid*, p. 7. The identification of these Four Malepas is a difficult question. Rice has conflicting accounts to give on the subject. In his earlier work—*Mysore Inscripitons*—he writes the following:—That during the long time which followed the capture of Talakāḍ by the Coḷas till the rise to power of the Hoysalas (*viz*., from A. D. 1004 till A. D. 1116)– which Rice reckoned to be 200 years !—nine brothers called Nava Daṇṇāyakas set up their principality in the Beṭṭadakoṭe on the Gopālaswāmi Hill (to the south west of Gunḍalpet tāluka) in the south of Mysore. The chief of the nine brothers was Perumāle Daṇṇāyaka.. Four brothers led by Bhīma Daṇṇāyaka quarrelled with the rest of the five and set up a separate principality at Nagarapura (Nañjanguḍ) and Ratnāpuri (Heḍatale). Some time later they returned to attack Beṭṭadakoṭe which fell by a strategem into their hands after a siege of three years. The defence of the citadel had been entrusted to Manca Daṇṇāyaka who, seeing the fall of the fort, mounted on a horse, leaped down the hill and was killed. The four victorious brothers placing a junior member of the family over the government of Beṭṭadakoṭe, set forth on their conquests in the course of which they penetrated as far as Goa in the north, Davasibeṭṭa (the southern point of Coorg) in the south, Bisale Ghat (in the north-west of Coorg) in the west, and Satyamaṅgalaṃ (on the Bhavānī in Coimbatore) in the east. These were the Male Rājas or Hill Chiefs and the Malepar whom the Hoysalas claimed to have subdued. *Mysore Inscriptions* Intr. pp. LXXVI-LXXVII.

But Rice contradicts himself in his account of the same chieftains as given in his *Mysore and Coorg from the Inscriptions*. While tracing the history of the Padinālkunāḍ, he mentions a Siṅgeya Daṇṇāyaka as one of the rulers of the principality in A. D. 1318. "Descendants from these were the Nava Daṇṇāyakas of tradition, nine brothers, identified with Beṭṭadakoṭe, the fort on the Gopālaswāmi hill, the chief of whom was Perumāl-daṇṇāyaka." And then Rice gives the story we have enumerated above. *Mysore and Coorg.*, pp. 153-4.

Now, the source of information for both these statements-*viz.*, that the Nava Daṇṇāyakas were the ancestors of the ruler Siṅgeya Daṇṇāyaka and that they were the descendants of that ruler-is tradition. Of these two assertions we are inclined to accept the former as valid. The Nava Daṇṇāyakas were anterior to Mādhava Daṇṇāyaka, the grandfather of Siṅgeya Daṇṇāyaka, on the following grounds:—

(a) We cannot conceive of nine brothers conquering that wide stretch of territory represented by Goa in the north and Devasibeṭṭa in the south in the fourteenth and fifteenth centuries without coming into conflict with the five famous brothers-Harihara, Bukka, Mārapa, Muddapa and Kampana-the founders of the great Vijayanagara Empire. The history of the conquests of these brothers makes no mention of the nine brothers. Therefore, the latter could only have belonged to an earlier age.

(b) If the Nava Dannāyakas had really belonged to the fourteenth century, we cannot explain one significant title which the Hoysalas appended when they rose to power in the eleventh century, *viz.*, *Maleparoḷ Gaṇḍān*, which was one of the most significant *birudus* of the Hoysala rulers.

(c) Finally, we know that in A. D. 977 there existed Four Malepas. This statement agrees admirably with the statement of tradition that long ago there were four brothers-the Four Daṇṇāyakas whose deeds have been eulogized in tradition.

These considerations compel us, therefore, to assign the Nava Daṇṇāyakas to the last quarter of the tenth century A. D.

77. Rice, *Mysore and Coorg.*, pp. 86, 95; *EC.* III. TN. 44, p. 76, text, p. 222.

78. *EC.* VII. Sk. 136, pp. 102 3.

79. *Ibid*, Sk. 99. p. 66.

80. *Ibid*, Sk. 99. pp. 68, text, p. 187.

81. Fleet, *Dyn. Kan. Dist.*, p. 65.

82. Rice, *ibid.* p. 94.

83. Rice, *Coorg Inscr.* p. 11. *EC.* VI. Intr. p. 14.

84. Rice, *Mysore and Coorg.*, pp. 86, 142.

85. For the story of how they came to be called Poy-Salas or Hoy-Salas, read, Rice, *ibid*, p. 95.

86. *Ibid*, pp. 86, 95.

87. On Nṛpa Kāma, read, *ibid*, p. 97.

88. *EC.* VI. Kd. 22, p. 5.

89. *EC.* IV. Kr. 49, p. 107.

90. *EC.* VI. Kd. 2, p. 1.

91. On the extent of his kingdom, read, Rice, *Mysore and Coorg.*, p. 98.

92. *EC.* III. Ml. 21, pp. 59, text, p. 177.

93. *EC.* V. Bl. 58, p. 57.

94. *EC.* III. Sr. 74, p. 25.

95. *Ibid*, TN. 31, p. 73.

96. *EC.* VII. Sh. 5, p. 10; *EC.* IV. Ng. 29, p. 118.

97. *EC.* III. Md. 121, p. 53; TN. 97, p. 86, text, p. 289.

98. *Ibid*, TN. 97, p. 80; *EC.* IV. Ch. 13, p. 2; Gu. 69. p. 48.

99. *EC.* II. No. 56, p. 142 (1st ed.).

100. *EC.* IV. Ng. 32, p. 120, text, p. 341.

101. *EC.* VI. Kd. 149, p. 29.

102. Rice, *Mysore Inscrp.* p., 329.

103. *Mysore Arch. Report* for 1916, p. 53. The name Malepa is met with so late as A. D. 1722 when the Mysore ruler Cikka Devendra is said to have defeated a great many enemies among whom were the Malepas (Malegas) on the west coast. *EC.* III. Sr. 64, p. 20.

104. *EC.* VII. Sk. 214, p. 129.

105. *Ibid,* Ci. 37, p. 184.

106. *EC.* VI. Kd. 148, p. 28.

107. *Ibid,* Tk. 84, p. 121.

108. *EC.* VII. Hl. 48, p. 169. The hill chiefs of the north have also figured in the history of the Panjab. Read Irvine, *Later Mughals,* I. p. 84 seq.

109. *EC.* VII. Ci. 53, p. 188.

110. *EC.* VI. Tk. 55, p. 113-4. On *Sameya-patra,* read, Saletore, *Social and Political Life.*, I. pp 171, 173, and 173, n. (2).

111. *EC.* XI. Dg. 38, p. 47.

112. Sewell, *A Forg. Empire,* p. 22, n.

113. *EC.* VIII. Nr. 29, pp. 131–2. See also Saletore, *ibid,* I. pp. 306, 319.

114. *Mys. Arch. Rept.* for 1925, pp. 14–5; Saletore, *ibid,* II. p. 54, n. (6).

115. Saletore, *ibid,* II. pp. 195-6. On the Beḍars in the history of the village organization of Beṭṭadapura, read *Mys. Arch. Report* for 1925, p. 14.

116. Saletore, *ibid,* I. 137–8.

117. *EC.* III. Hl. 6 and 7, p. 116. See also *ibid,* Intr p. 29.

118. *Bellary Gazetteer,* p. 249.

119. For a full account of the rulers, read *EC.* IX. Intr. pp. 28–9; *Mysore Gazt.* II. p. 501 seq. (rev. ed).

120. Rice, *Mysore and Coorg.*, pp. 159 60.

121. *EC.* VII. Sk. 210, pp. 128–9.

122. Rice, *Mysore and Coorg.*, p. 162; *EC.* IX. Intr. p. 28; *Mysore Arch. Rep.* for 1929, p. 22.

123. Sharma, *QJMS.* XX. pp. 2, 94, 100, 104. The Beḍars have figured in the history of Ceylon where they were called Veddahs. The Veddah method of discharging arrows with the aid of pressure from the left foot on the extremity of the bow resting on the ground, may be compared to an identical method used by the infantry in the Mauryan times. It is not improbable that there were Beḍars in the Mauryan army too. Read Smith, *Oxford History of India*, p. 64 (1920) where reference is given to Tennent, *Ceylon*, I. p. 499.

124. Manucci, *Storia do Mogor*, II. cited by Prof. Sen. *Military System of the Mahrattas*, pp. 87–8. (Calcutta, 1928).

125. Sen, *ibid.*

126. Manucci, *ibid.*

127. *Basava Purāṇa* Ch. 18, 9, 36; Murdoch, *Catalogue of Classified Tamil Books*, p. 77; Taylor, *Cat. Rais.* III. pp. 457–8; *EC.* IV. Intr. p. 37; *Mys. Arch. Report for 1925*, p. 7.

128. *Mys. Arch. Report for 1913–4*, p. 19.

129. *Ibid*, for 1917, p. 20.

130 & 131. *Ibid for 1918*, pp. 14, 17.

132. Rice, *Kanarese Literature*, p. 59. (1st ed).

133. Taylor, *Cat. Rais.* III. p. 408. An instance of a *Sati* by a Beḍar woman is recorded in a defaced record of the times of the Hoysala king Vīra Ballāḷa III. *Mys. Arch. Report for 1928*, p. 88.

CHAPTER V

MISCELLANEOUS TRIBES

1. *Ptolemy*, VII. 1. 64; IA. LI. p. 219; Oppert, *MJLS* for 1886, pp. 114–5.

2. Geiger–Bode, *Mahāvamso*, p. 50. and *ibid.*, n. (5).

3. *Rāmāyaṇa*, Kiṣkindha kaṇḍa, XLI. 17.

4. *Sabhā Parva*, XXIX. p. 84. It may have been the Pulindas who spread in the east. These were found around Magadha. Read *IA*. XLVII. p. 299. On some notices of the Pulindas, see *IA*. for 1923, p. 24 seq.

5. *Sabhā Parva*, XXXI. p. 88.

6. *Bhīṣma Parva*, IX. p. 32.

7 & 8. *Viṣṇu Purāṇa*, pp. 186, *ibid*, n. (15), 123.

9. *Mārkaṇḍeya Purāṇa*, p. 335; *Garuḍa Purāṇa*, Ch. 55, v. 13, p. 140 (Calcutta, 1890).

10–12. *Matsya Purāṇa*, pp. 309, 327.

13. *Bṛihatsaṁhitā*, IV. 32; V. 39, 77–8; IX. 17, 29, 40; XVI. 2, 33.

14. Bühler, *Zeitschrift der deutschen Morgenländischen Gesellschaft*. XL. p. 138. This error was repeated by Fleet, *IA*. XVII. p. 187, and again in *ibid*, XXII. p. 187, and by Smith, *EHI*. p. 184, n. (2). Dr. Bimala Churn Law unfortunately accepts it. *Indian Culture* I. p. 384, 390. Dr. Law identifies Pulindanagara with Rupanath. *ibid*, p. 383,

15 Hultzsch, *Cor. Insc. Ind.* I. p. 48, and *ibid*, n. (14).

16. & 17. Sharma, *QJMS*. XX. p. 90-1, 101.

18. *Cennabasava Purāṇa*, 6, 48, 49 cited by Kittel in his edition of Nāgavarma's *Cchandas*. pp. 133-4. Mangalore, 1875.

19. Burgess-Sastri, *Tamil and Sanskrit Inscriptions*, I. p. 1135. We may note that Pulinda or Pulina was the name of Bāṇa's son who finished the *uttarabhāga* of the *Kādambarī*. S. R. Bhandarkar, *Report on the search for Sanskrit Mss.* for 1904-6, p. 39.

20. *Kavicarite*, II. pp. 247-8. Oppert quotes a verse from the *Pārās'urāpaddhati* which mentions the Bhills, the Pulindas, the Pullas, the Mallas, etc. In this connection he has some pertinent remarks to make concerning the conjectures of Cunningham. Read *MJLS* for 1886, pp 110, 112, and 112 n. (70).

21. *Manu*, X. 8, *18*. 48.

22. *Garuḍa Purāṇa*, Chs. VI. v. 6, LV. v. 15, pp. 16, 140.

23. *Harivaṁs'a*, XV. v. 27; XXXIV. v. 33; XCIV. v. 32.

24. On Rudradāman's inscriptions, read Burgess, *ASW*. I, pp. 43, 129, 130-131; J. B. R. A. S. VIII, pp. 234-5; Law, *Ancient Indian Tribes*, II. p. 63.

25. Pargiter, *Dynasties of the Kali Age*, p. 54. See also Jayaswal, *History of India*, pp. 124-131; Law, *Ancient Indian Tribes*, II. p. 63.

26. *Vivekacintāmaṇi*, pp 422-3. See also Kittel, *ibid*, p. 134. Dr. Law's attempt to distinguish the Niṣādas from the Niṣadhas (*Ancient Indian Tribes*, II. pp. 61-63) is, in my opinion, difficult to be followed. B. A. S.

27. Fausböll, *Jātakas*, No. 514.

28. Lassen, *Indische Altertumskunde*, III. pp. 235-7.

29. McCrindle, *Ptolemy* pp. 70-1. See also McCrindle, *Ancient India*, p. 198, ns. (7) & (8). (London, 1901).

30. Gerini, *Ptolemy*, pp. 116-7, 126.

31. Rāmāyaṇa, *Kiṣkindha kaṇḍa*, XLI. 9, p. 1606 (Mudholkar, Bombay, 1912).

32. Sewell, *Lists.*, II. p. 141.

33. *Virāṭa Parva*, I. p. 2. In the same epic we are told that S'ikhaṇḍin married the daughter of the king of Das'ārṇa named Hiraṇyavarman. *Udyoga Parva*, Ch. 190, p. 544.

34. *Sabhā Parva*, XXIX. p. 84, XXXII. p. 93.

35. *Bhīṣma Parva*, IX. p. 32; L. p. 186. See also *Viṣṇu Purāṇa*, II. p. 159, n. where it is said that in the Bengal recension of the Rāmāyaṇa, *Kiṣkindhā kanda* XLI. 9, the Kukuras are mentioned immediately after the Das'ārṇas as a southern people. (Wilson).

36. *Viṣṇu Purāṇa* pp. 186, 192.

37. *Mārkaṇḍeya Purāṇa*, pp. 296, 341–2, 360. On p. 360, n. Pargiter opines that the Das'ārnas were "altogether out of place here".

38. Kauṭalaya *Arthas'āstra*, Bk. II. Ch. II. p. 54.

39. *Matsya Purāṇa*, I. pp. 308-310. Here the *Matsya Purāṇa* relates that the Mandākinī, the Das'ārṇa, the Citrakūṭa, the Tāmasā, and other rivers have their source in the Ṛṣyamūkha mountains. *Ibid*, I. Ch. CXIV. vv. 20-32, p. 308. Pargiter assumes that the Mandākinī, the Das'ārṇa, and the Tāmasā rise in the Vindhyas, while the S'oṇa, the Mahānadī, and the Narmadā rise in the Ṛkṣa mountains. *Mārk. Purāṇa*, p. 298, n.

40. *Harivaṁs'a*, Ch. XXIV. v. 20, XXXIX vv. 10-20.

41. *Bṛhatsaṁhitā*, V. 40, X. 15, XIV. 8-10, XVI 26, XXX. 11. The *Bhāgavata Purāṇa* also mentions the *Das'ārṇa* country but calls the Das'ārṇa people Das'ārha. I., 11, 11,; II, 14, 23; III. 1, 29; X. 45, 15; X. 47, 44; X. 78, 39; XI. 30, 18.

42-44. *Meghadūta*, Purv. vv. 24, 25, 28.

45. Cunningham, *Stupa of Barhut*, p. 132 (1879).

46. Pargiter, *Mārk. Purāṇa*, pp. 296, and *ibid*, n., 297, and *ibid*. n. According to Pargiter, Vidis'ā appears to be the modern Bhilsa itself. *Ibid*, p. 295, n.

47. *Viṣṇu Purāṇa*, pp. 186, n. (17) 187.

48. Rājākānta Deva Bahadūr, *S'abdakalpadruma*, VI. p. 696.

49. *EC*. VII. Sk. 136, p. 101.

50. *The Sources of Vijayanagara History*, *Sāluvābhyudayam*, Canto, VI. pp. 91, 94, 98.

51. *IA*. III. p. 224.

52. *Rāmāyaṇa*, Araṇya kaṇḍa, LXXVII, vv. 19-21, pp. 313-4
53. *JRAS* for 1894, pp. 253-4.
54. *Vana Parva* , LXXXIV. p. 272.
55. *Matsya Purāṇa*, I. p. 319.
56. *Bṛhatsaṁhitā*, LXXX, p. 7.
57. Cowell, The *Jātaka* or Stories of the Buddha's Former Births. IV. p. 235. (Cambridge, 1895)
58. *Cariyapīṭaka* p. 19. (B. C. Law, Lahore, 1924)
59. *Raghuvaṁs'a*, V. 53.
60. *Kādambarī*, Purv. p. 8.(Ridding).
61. *Das'akumāracarita*, pp. 126-7, op. cit.
62. *IA*. V. op. 71-2, VIII, p. 243; Rice, *Mysore Gaz*. I. p. 321 (1st. ed); *Mysore* and *Coorg*, p. 63.
63. *EC*. IX. Dg. 1, p. 21.
64. & 65. *IA*. V. p. 72, & *ibid*, n.
65. *JRAS* for 1910, p. 429 seq.; See also *QJMS*, III. p. 63.
69. *Das'akumāracarita*, Ucch. VIII. pp. 200-204.
68. *JRAS* for 1910, p. 447.

69. On Māhiṣmatı, read, Kālidāsa, *Raghuvaṁs'a*, VI. 42-44; *Harivaṁs'a*, XXXIII. 1-16; XCIV; A southern Māhiṣmatī is mentioned in the *Mahā-Bhārata* as having been conquered by Sahadeva after beholding the celebrated caves of Kiṣkindhyā. *Sabhā Parva*, XXXI, pp. 88-9. Wilson identified the southern Māhiṣmatı with Culi Maheswar on the Narmadā, *Viṣṇu Purāṇa*, p. 189, n. (54). Fleet rejected this for Māndhāta an island in the same river. *JRAS* for 1910, p. 447. See also Rice, *Mysore Inscr*. Intr. p. xxviii; *IA* VI. pp. 79-80; LI. p. 219; *EI*. IV. p. 86 n. (5). On Māhiṣmatımaṇḍala and Mysore, see Saletore, *Social and Political Life*, I. p. 40, n. (2).

70. There were the Kaḷacuriyas of Kalañjara, a hill fortress in modern Bundelkand; those of Tripura, modern Tewar, a village about six miles to the west of Jabalpūr ; and the later Kaḷacuriyas. Fleet, *Dyn. Kan. Dist*. p. 57 seq. Rice takes no

notice of the early Kaḷacuriyas at all but starts with Kṛṣṇa. *Mysore and Coorg*, p. 78 seq.

71. *EC*. V. Cn. 179, p. 203.

72. *EC*. VII. Hn. 8, p. 159.

73. *EC*. XII Pg. 53, p. 125.

74. Sharma, *QJMS*. XX. pp. 201-211.

75. Taylor, *Cat. Rais*. III. p. 180 ; Saletore, *ibid*, I. p. 114.

76. *Mysore Arch. Report for 1929* p. 169.

77. *33 of the Madras Epigraphical Report for 1901* ; *South Indian Inscriptions*, VII. No. 202, p. 95, line 13.

78. Sewell, *Lists*. I. p. 174.

79. *Mysore Arch. Report for* 1918, p. 14.

80. *Madras Epigraphical Report for* 1921, p. 7. Oppert writes that *S'yāmalā-daṇḍaka*, ascribed to Kālidāsa, contains a *s'loka* concerning Mātaṅgi. *MJLS* for 1886-7, p. 45, n.

81. *Garuḍa Purāṇa*, Ch. 68, vv. 17, seq, p. 173 seq. (Calcutta, 1890); Oldham, JBORS, XII, p. 197.

82 & 83. *JASB* for 1873, No. 187; *IA*. III. p. 178. Pargiter gave the following as the boundaries of the kingdom of the Puṇḍras : They had the Kās'is on their north; the Aṅgas, the Vaṅgas, and the Suhmas on their north-east; and the Oḍras on their south-west. Hence their territory corresponded to modern Chota Nagpur with the exceptions of the southern portions. Their boundary on the south was no doubt the land of the Utkalas. The territory of the Puṇḍras extended to the Chambal river. *Mārkaṇḍeya Purāṇa* p. 327, n.

84. B. C. Law, *Indian Historical Quarterly*, XII. pp. 1349–353 ; Ancient Indian Tribes, II. pp. 16-17.

85. *Ādi Parva*, CIV. 4217–21. Cf. *Harivaṁs'a*, where Puṇḍra and Kaliṅga are said to be Kṣatriya sons of Bali. Ch. XXXVI vv. 34–35.

86 & 87. *Mārkaṇḍeya Purāṇa*, pp. 329, n ; 331, and *ibid*, n.

88 & 89. *Bṛhatsaṁhitā*, XIV. 6 7; XVI. 3, pp. 88, 100

90. *Mys. Arch. Report* for 1921, p. 21.

91. *Ibid* for 1919, p. 29.

92. *EC.* IX. Dg. 41, p. 52.

93. *EC.* VI. Kd. 51, p. 11.

94. *Pliny*, II. Bk. VII, Ch. 2, p. 134.

95. Geiger-Bode *Mahāvamso*, pp. 247-9

96. Read, *ibid*, 247 seq.; 260 seq. Codrington, *A Short History of Ceylon*, p. 29. (London, 1926.)

97. Mandeville, *Travels*, p. 134

98. Nāgavarma, *Kannaḍa Cchandas*, p. 22, n. (1).

99. Wilson, *Viṣṇu Purāṇa*, p. 187, n. (22)

100. Mandeville, *ibid*.

101. McCrindle, *Ancient India as described in Classical Literature*, p. 62.

102. *Sabhā Parva*, III. p. 145.

103. Ibid, XXXI. p. 92. What relationship these Karnapravarṇas had with the Karṇasuvarṇas of eastern India, cannot be made out. S'as'āṅka, king of Karṇasuvarṇa in eastern India, and the contemporary and murderer of Rājyavardhana II of Kanouj, is mentioned by Hiuen Tsiang as a persecutor of Buddhists. Beal, *Buddhist, Records*, I. p. 210 seq; II. pp. 42, 91, 118 & 121; Fleet, *Cor. Insr. Ind.* III. p. 284.

104. Rāmayaṇa, *Kiṣkindha kaṇḍa*, XL.

105. Gerini, *Ptolemy*, p. 256, n. (1). Read also *ibid*, pp. 160–162.

106. McCrindle, *India as described by Megasthenes and Arrian*, pp. 75-6; *Ancient India as described in Classical Literature*, p. 62. and *ibid*, n.(3).

107. *Pliny*, 11, Bk. 11. Ch. 2, p. 130.

108. *Sabhā Parva*, LI. 142.

109. *Ibid*, XXI, p. 92.

110 & 111. *Mārkaṇḍeya Purāna*, pp. 358, 383.

112. *Bṛhatsaṁhitā*. XIV. 5-7.

113. Mandeville, *Travels*, p. 134. Certain tribes recall the Ekapādas. These are the Toḍas of the Niligiris. Read Rice, *Mys. Inscr.* pp. xxxvi, 123, 222. see also N. G. Ranga, *The Tribes of the Niligiris.* (Andhra Economic Series, Bezwada. 1933 (?))

114. Mandeville, *ibid*, p. 133.

115. *Mārkaṇḍeya Purāṇa*, p. 374.

116. *EC.* VII. Sk. 118, p. 86. This inscription is dated in A. D. 1054 in the *Mys. Inscr.* p. 123.

117. *EC.* V. Bl. 3, p. 45. This record is dated in circa 1380. *Mys. Inscr.* p. 222.

118. Risley, *Castes and Tribes of Bengal*, I. p. 490; Pargiter *Mārkaṇḍeya Purāṇa*, p. 322, 335, op. cit.

119. *Matsya Purāṇa*, P. I. p. 327, op. cit.

120–122 *Bhagavat Gītā*, X. 23; XI. 22; XVII. 4.

123. Cannibalism does not seem to have died out altogether from the Pais'āca country, according to the opinion of some. Read *JRAS* for 1905.

124. Cowell, *The Jataka.*, VI. pp. 46–47.

125. *Ibid*, III. p. 97.

126. *Ibid*, V. p. 18.

127. *Ibid*, V. p. 51.

128. *Ibid*, III. p. 106.

129. *Ibid*, p. 132.

130. Geiger-Bode, *Mahāvamso*, p. 262.

131. Cowell, *ibid*, III, p. 298.

132 & 133. Geiger-Bode *ibid*, pp. 56–7.

134. *Ibid*, pp. 72–73.

135 & 136. *Ibid*, pp. 3–4, 57.

137. *Cariyapīṭika*, p. 20.

138. Cowell, *ibid*, III. pp. 96–97.

139–142. Kalhaṇa, *Rājataraṅgiṇī*, I. vv. 159, 184, 319, pp. 29, 33, 48; III. v. 349, p. 102. (Stein's trans.)

143. *Meghadūta*, Purv. I, 1.

144. *Das'akumāracarita*, Purv. p. 19. This Tārāvalī,

daughter of Maṇibhadra, again appears in Ucch. IV, pp. 126–27.

145. *Ibid*, Ucch. IV. pp. 39; Ucch. VII. p. 178.

146. Abhinava Pampā, *Rāmāyaṇa*. VII. 127.

147. Cowell, *The Jātaka*., VI. p. 43.

148. *Ibid*, IV. p. 159. Cf. Kādambari, III, p. 194, seq. where Bāṇa describes Candrāpīḍa enchanted by the music of a pair of Kinnaras. (Kane, Bombay. 1914)

149. Cunningham, *Barhut Stupa* Pl. XXVII, p. 5; *IHQ*, X, p. 347.

150. Cowell, *ibid*, III. p. 259.

151. *Ibid*, VI. p. 217. A Kinnara ascetic is also introduced in the *Khadirangara Jātaka*, as advising in vain a great merchant named Anāthapiṇḍika against giving charity to the Boddhisattva. *Ibid*, I. p. 100.

152. Fausböll, *Jātaka*, No. 485.

153. *IHQ*. X. pp. 344–347.

154 & 155. *Meghadūta*, Purv. 59; Uttar. 10.

156. *Kādambari*, Purv. v. 351, p. 143, (Ridding). See also Kāne's ed. p 55

It is regretted that some of the best editions of a few of the Sanskrit works referred to above, were inaccessible to me while writing the book. I had access to them only when the major part of the Ms. had passed through the press. B. A. S.

INDEX

B

N

†

Select Opinions on the

SOCIAL AND POLITICAL LIFE IN THE VIJAYANAGARA EMPIRE

BY

Dr. B. A. Saletore, M. A., Ph. D.

Dr. L. D. Barnett, British Museum, London, writes :—"...I heartily congratulate you on the publication of the work, and cordially thank you for doing me the honour of inscribing my name on the page of dedication..."

John Allan, British Museum, London, writes :—"...It is an admirable summing up of all the sources presented in a readable fashion...an excellent piece of work..."

Luzac's Oriental List for 1934 :—"...One of the most useful works on Indian History that has appeared for a considerable time...this sweeping survey ... is a work of constructive scholarship, in which the raw materials have been transmuted so as to form a live picture of an age which in some respects was one of the greatest in the long panorama of Indian history..."

Professor Benoy Kumar Sarkar, Calcutta, writes:—"...Since ... ... two decades ago, we have been used to look upon South Indian Scholarship as a dynamic factor in the remaking of our knowledge regarding Hindu Culture. Dr.

in this work which may be described as one of capital importance ... This work...has enriched the historical literature on India. ... We have here a fine book, the production of fine scholarship ... On the whole, it is a real scholarly work, bearing the stamp of the best distinction, and we can congratulate the author on this fine production; and we hope that many more of this kind are to come from him in the future."

The Indian Culture, Calcutta, in its July issue, 1934 :— "...the wealth of details with which he has enriched his narrative is truly amazing and deserves special recognition ...these...excellent volumes..."

Dr. R. C. Majumdar, Dacca University, writes :—"...The book is a monument of industry and scholarship...These magnificent volumes give a comprehensive review of the life of the people under the famous Empire of Vijayanagara, and are a distinct contribution to our knowledge of the medieaval history of India..."

The Times of India, Bombay, in its Literary Supplement dated 25th of May 1934, writes :— "... a detailed and exhaustive study..."

Journal of the Bombay Branch of the Royal Asiatic Society, N. S. Vol. X., 1934 :— "... His attempt is the first of its kind in bringing before the reader classical and mediaeval Hindu theory in harmony with Vijayanagara maxims and practice ... we congratulate Dr. Saletore on the success achieved by him in his enterprise ... ".

Henry Heras, S. J., M. A., Bombay, writes in his letter of 5th March 1934 :— " ...This is a very creditable achievement of yours, indeed...my heartiest congratulations..."

The Journal of Indian History, Madras, April, 1934, writes :- "...a voluminous and detailed study of the political and social institutions of the Empire of Vijayanagara..."

The Hindu, Madras, in its issue of 9th May 1934 :— "...Dr. Saletore's work deserves to be warmly welcomed by all serious students of South Indian History."

The same author's forthcoming book

History of Early Tuluva

INTRODUCTORY

History of India from the pre-Mahabharata War down to 320-348 A. D. (the beginning of the Gupta Period) is chronicled in the *Puranas*. For the subsequent period we have been dependent on inscriptions; and it had been believed that there was no text or written history for it. The inscriptions left certain 'blanks', and gave us a fragmentary view. It is therefore a matter of no small satisfaction to recover a text which turns out to give a connected history where we needed it most. And what is still more gratifying is the Imperial feature of that history. Some of the matters of great importance that this written record discloses are:—

(1) a full and complete history of the IMPERIAL GUPTA epoch (348 A. D. to 500 A. D.), describing its break-up(500 A. D),

(2) imperial history from (*a*) VISHNUVARDHANA (520–535 A. D.), then following the (*b*) imperial family of the MAUKHARIS (555-600 A. D.) down to (*c*) his descendants' re-rise in the person of Prabhakaravardhana and HARSHAVARDHANA (606–647 A. D.), [with a full history of Sasanka, who was a Brahmin by caste and a popular leader rising from Bengal].

(3) history of a REVIVED GUPTA EMPIRE, following the death of Harshavardhana, with its decline and fall,

(4) then a vivid description of two popular elections of kings in Bengal and the rise of Gopala.

Numerous important details, e. g., that MAHAPADMA NANDA had been the Prime Minister of Magadha before his kingship, that there was a short-lived *republic* in Bengal after Sasanka–come in as additions to our knowledge. Further, Indian Imperial history for the first time receives personal touches when the author gives his estimate of character of individual emperors. All this welcome information is stored in a long section–which is a book by itself, being in 1000 ślokas–in the Mahayana work entitled *Arya-Manjusri-Mulakalpa*, published (Part III) in the year 1925 by the late MM. Ganapati Shastri.

Possibly some of the Indian scholars, trained to suspect every written book in Sanskrit, would have darkly hinted that 'the book was a 'Southern forgery'.'. But fortunately the book was translated in Tibetan in the eleventh century A. D. and the present text agrees word for word with that translation.

Bhadanta Rahula Sankrityayana has collected a unique library from Tibet, including an original Sanskrit manuscript which had been taken from India and translated there. He was fortunate enough to obtain a complete set of Buston's works from the Dalai Lama, which is not available even in the rich Russian collection. With the help and co-operation of Rev. Sankrityayana and his valuable Tibetan library, the learned author has been able to compare the text of Manjusri-Mulakalpa with the Tibetan text and to derive benefit from Buston (b. 1289 A. D.-d. 1363 A. D.) for the purpose of following some passages and obtaining additional light on the history of SKANDA GUPTA.

According to the Manjusri-Mulakalpa, **Indian history is a succession of empires from the time preceding the Buddha to c. 750 A. D.** where it stops. To take the period from 78 A. D., it consists of the following successions:

(a) *Saka dynasty* (*Sakavamsa, i. e.,* Kushans)

(b) *Naga-Senas,* or *Nagas* and *Prabha-Visnu, i. e.,* Vishnu-vriddha Pravara-sena (Vakataka),

(c) Guptas (up to Buddha Gupta),

(d) Vishnu (vardhana) and one descendant,

(e) Maukharis,

(f) *Srikantha* dynasty, [Aditya (vardhana), Rajya (vardhana) etc.],

(g) Imperial Valabhi dynasty (two generations),

(h) Imperial '*Gauda dynasty*' i. e. Later Guptas: Adityasena to Vishnu-Gupta.

It will be atonce noticed that (d), (e) and (g) go to fill up blanks in Indian History.

Thus it is clear from the above facts that the present Imperial History of India by Mr. K. P. Jayaswal is a unique one.